THE SHEPHERD'S GUIDEBOOK

Practical Guidance for Pastors
Called to Lead with Character,
Integrity and Discernment

LAMBERT W. GATES, SR.

The Shepherd's Guidebook: Practical Guidance for Pastors Called to Lead with Character, Integrity and Discernment

Copyright © 2025 by Lambert W. Gates, Sr.

All rights reserved. No part of this book may be reproduced, stored in a retrieval system, or transmitted in any form or by any means, electronic, mechanical, photocopying, recording, or otherwise, without prior written permission from the publisher.

For permissions or bulk orders, please contact:
L.W. Gates Ministries
4900 E. 38th Street
Indianapolis, IN 46218

ISBN: 979-8-9929969-1-3

All Scripture quotations are taken from the New King James Version®. Copyright © 1982 by Thomas Nelson. Used by permission. All rights reserved.

Table of Contents

Introduction 9
LEADERSHIP 19
    Honoring the Past While Embracing Growth 21
    The Need for Critical Thinking 22
    Passing the Torch Without Restriction 24
    Leadership Success in the Kingdom 25
THE BUSINESS OF THE CHURCH 29
    Operating the Church Like the Business It Is 31
    Handling Transparency and Accountability
    with Church Finances 32
    Managing Church Growth and
    Financial Sustainability 34
    Tools and Systems of Organization 36
    Keeping the Church Focused on Vision 36
    Realigning People to the Vision 37
THE MINISTRY LEADER 39
    The Leader's Call 41
    Being Sure of the Call 42
    Developing a Culture of Honor for the Leader 43
    Defining Success in Your Ministry Assignment 44
    Surrendering Plans and Preferences
    for God's Purpose 45

Keeping Your Fire Burning 46
Keeping a Connection to Mentors 48
The Leader's Preparation 49
Staying Sensitive to the Leading of the Holy Spirit ... 50
Including the Holy Spirit in Decision-Making 51
Discerning God's Will in Difficult Seasons 53
Developing a Personal Study Routine 53
Keeping Sermons Fresh and Relevant 55
Balancing Inspiration and Information 56
Speaking on Social & Justice Issues 57
Evaluating Effectiveness as a Preacher 59

GROWING, DISCIPLING & SHEPHERDING CONGREGANTS 61
Growing Spiritually Mature Members 63
Advancing an Evangelism Strategy 64
Empowering Members to Witness 65
Supporting Young People in Faith Formation 66
Staying Connected to Members' Real Needs 67
Training Others in Congregational Care 68

FAMILY MATTERS 71
Child Abuse 73
Pastoral Discretion and Legal Awareness 74
Domestic Violence 75
Infidelity 75
Divorce 77

Addiction 78

LGBTQ+ Issues 82

CONFLICT RESOLUTION AND CHURCH HURT 87

Recognizing and Addressing Conflict 89

The Spiritual Reality of Conflict 90

Understanding Contrast vs. Conflict 91

Managing Conflict Within the Church 92

Church Hurt & the Perception
of Being Overlooked 92

PASTORS' MATTERS 97

Attacks on the Pastor 99

Handling Criticism 100

Handling Conflict Biblically 102

Processing Hard Questions from
Church Members 103

Balancing Family and Ministry 105

Understanding & Avoiding Nepotism 108

Managing Stress 111

Overcoming Burnout & Taking Sabbaticals 113

Seeking Counseling and Support 116

Protecting Your Heart in Ministry 117

Setting Boundaries in Pastoral Relationships 118

Maintaining Respectable Character 120

Battling Addiction 121

Setting Up Accountability 122

  Recovering and Responding After
  Making Mistakes 124

CHURCH MATTERS 127

  Transitioning Members Out of and Into
  the Congregation 129

  Healthy Church Growth 130

  Balancing Growth with Intimacy and Connection . 131

  Overcoming Church Growth Obstacles 133

  The Importance of Radical Hospitality 135

  Training Members and Leaders
  to Extend Hospitality 136

  Creating a Culture of Worship 137

  Identifying and Equipping New Leaders 140

  Leadership Development 141

  Dealing with Leadership Gaps 142

  Delegating Responsibility 143

  Maintaining Unity Within the Team 144

  Incorporating Young Adults Into
  the Church's Future 146

  Developing and Empowering the
  Next Generation of Leaders 147

THE CHURCH IN THE COMMUNITY 149

  Interaction with Other Congregations 151

  Staying Engaged with Your Community 152

  Building Bridges with Local Leaders 154

FINALLY, MY BRETHREN 155

Dedication

To the faithful shepherds—past, present, and yet to come—
who lead not for applause, but by divine assignment;
who carry the flock with bowed knees and lifted eyes.
Your labor is not in vain.

To my beloved wife, my children, and my grandchildren—
your love steadies my soul and sanctifies my steps.

To the spiritual fathers and mentors
whose wisdom shaped the well I now draw from—
this is fruit of your planting.

To the assistants who lift quietly,
and the editor who gave form to the fire—
this is our shared offering.

INTRODUCTION

THE WEIGHT AND WONDER OF PASTORAL LEADERSHIP

Let's talk about what it really means to be a pastor. Pastoral ministry is one of the most sacred responsibilities a person can accept. Souls are literally entrusted to our care, and the wisdom, counsel, and direction we provide play a significant role in shaping lives. Paul made this clear when he instructed Timothy, "Lay hands on no man suddenly" (1 Timothy 5:22).

Pastoral leadership requires maturity, wisdom, and deep commitment. It's not a position to be assumed lightly. But here's the challenge: we live in a world that prizes speed and instant success. There's pressure to move forward quickly, to build something fast, to accomplish more and more. Sometimes, in that rush, we bypass the necessary process that actually prepares us for the calling. I say it often: we've become so obsessed with destiny that we fail to embrace the process. But let me tell you, the process is where wisdom is gained, where leadership is refined, where character is shaped. Ministry is not just about stepping into a role. It's about becoming the leader God intends you to be along the way.

Experience plays a vital role in shaping a pastor, but that doesn't mean you have to be old to be wise. What matters most is that sobriety and preparation accompany the transition into pastoral leadership. I remember when I first stepped into the role of pastor and I used to joke with my congregation, "My name might be on the sign, but I'm not really your pastor yet!" Truthfully, my pastor, Bishop James Nelson Sr., was still guiding me, mentoring me, providing oversight. Any major decision I made in those first years went before him because I understood the weight of pastoral responsibility. I feared making the wrong move. That kind of wisdom comes from recognizing that leadership requires accountability.

Accountability truly matters in your role as a pastor. These days, it's too easy to let ministry become about prestige or personal recognition to the point that young or newer pastors may tend to shun the idea of being accountable to a veteran ministry leader. However, what God has called pastors to do requires so much more than we are capable of understanding, figuring out, or processing ourselves. You need someone to hold you accountable, serving as your mentor, covering and wise counselor if you will operate effectively and succeed in this role.

Pastoral ministry is not just about influence; it's about souls… and souls are complex. You're not going to be able to figure them out by yourself without making a lot of unnecessary mistakes. They require patience, love, and discernment, so as a pastor, you must not simply tolerate people, but genuinely love them. In many ways, you'll find that pastoral ministry requires the instincts of an uncredentialed psychologist, because leadership demands an understanding of personalities, temperaments, and human nature. Paul said, "I became all things to all men, that by all means I might win some" (1 Corinthians 9:22). This is not just referring to preaching in different places; it's about knowing how to reach people where they are, while staying anchored in biblical truth. As a pastor, preparation, training, and mentorship will be vital in helping you to do this.

You may already know this, but preaching is only one part of the job; pastoring is about genuinely caring for people, walking with them, watching for them, praying for their families, investing in them, bearing their burdens, and so much more. It is also about continuing to function in this role of care and covering when they don't seem to appreciate you, when they reject your wise counsel, when they don't show up, and even when they hurt you. When I install young men and women into pastoral leadership, I remind them of something Bishop Nelson told me early on: "Sometimes, you have to let the sheep walk on you!" That means embracing the sacrificial love that Christ modeled when He said, "The good shepherd lays down His life for the sheep" (John 10:11).

Scripture tells us to "stir up the gift" (2 Timothy 1:6). There is a gifting that comes with pastoral ministry, and it is an ability to love people deeply. However, that gift must be cultivated. You don't just wake up knowing how to shepherd and guide the sheep; you must learn how to do it through training and mentorship. You must grow to do it better every day. You must refine your calling. You must want to become the best pastor you can possibly be for the spiritual growth and development of the souls that have been entrusted to your care.

There are people who enter ministry without any pastoral instincts, which raises the question: Were they truly called? I cannot emphasize enough that the first qualification for pastoring is an unwavering love for people, followed by a willingness to sacrifice for them. It involves valuing souls so deeply that you are willing to make the necessary sacrifices to lead them well.

However, be warned that as much as you desire to be a better pastor, to grow in love and genuine care and concern for your flock, and to invest in yourself through training, study and mentorship, there are spiritual forces that will oppose you on every side. Despite your pure heart and good intentions to lay down your life to lead God's people, conflict will abound. Do not let this be a surprise; let it be an expectation for which you prepare yourself spiritually.

A part of leading well means knowing when to step back from unnecessary conflict. Believe it or not, the very people that you sacrifice and lay down your life to lead will fight you the whole way! Don't allow this to deter or discourage you. Paul talks about those who "oppose themselves" (2 Timothy 2:25). Sometimes, pastors struggle with opposition because they don't recognize the deeper spiritual battle at play. Ministry isn't about fighting with people; it's about guiding them toward healing and wholeness. You can't afford to get caught in personality conflicts and distractions. Your role is to rise above it, model integrity, and keep your focus on the work God has called you to do. He's called you to love the people He has placed under your care unconditionally and, despite the way they treat you and the ministry, watch for their souls.

If you are stepping into this calling without the willingness to lay aside personal comfort for the sake of shepherding souls, you may need to reconsider whether you are truly prepared for this work, because it is going to test every part of your being! Ministry will stretch you. It will require sacrifice, and the challenges you face will evolve with each passing year. In fact, regardless of how long you function in the role of pastor, the challenges will never end. Ever. They just take on new forms as the times and people change. Thus, you're going to need some help!

One of the most important things for pastors to remember is that ministry is a challenge and a struggle for everyone, regardless of tenure or preparation, but it is not a journey meant to be taken alone. If you are leading others and struggling with the realities, pressures, and frustrations of ministry, let me assure you, you are surrounded by other men and women who are having the same experiences. You are not alone! Further, not only are there other people who are going through what you are going through, but there are many other people who have been where you are. This is where every pastor benefits from having mentors that they can go to when things get difficult. They've been there and done what you are trying to do, and they can share some critical keys to helping you navigate situations they've already survived.

If you are a more established pastor with some experience under your belt, I encourage you to make yourself available to the younger pastors struggling on their journey. Every generation needs mentorship, yet many leaders get so caught up in the work that they neglect the next generation of pastors. The Apostle Paul told Timothy in 2 Timothy 2:2 that we must pass down what we have learned to others. That means established pastors need to invest time in developing future leaders, and young pastors need to recognize their need for guidance.

The truth is, every pastor needs a pastor. Leading without accountability, or someone to provide wise counsel and guidance for critical decisions is dangerous, both for the leader and for the church. The pastoral office does not make you superhuman; it simply gives you a different responsibility. Just as you watch over the souls of others, someone needs to be watching over you. Don't try to do this without a pastoral covering.

Ministry is no different from any other profession in this regard. In the world, there are apprenticeships in every skilled trade, in which more established veteran tradesmen train the newer up-and-coming workers to ensure they master the art of the craft before venturing out on their own. Why would pastoral ministry be any different? We are not just managing an organization; we are stewarding souls, which is a *much* more critical responsibility! If you are a pastor, the stakes are too high for you to go at it alone, thinking *I've got this on my own* rather than submitting yourself to a pastoral covering, mentorship, and ongoing preparation and training. If you enter ministry believing you already have all the answers, it is because you have failed to grasp the true gravity of your assignment. The fear of the Lord must shape every decision you make, and you must approach your assignment with humility rather than pride.

When I was younger and getting started as a ministry leader, I often thought about how helpful it would be to have a resource available to me that laid out the challenges of pastoral leadership, including the real struggles, the weight of responsibility, and advice on how to handle the hard situations. That is why I wrote this book. I wrote it to equip you and to answer the questions lingering in your heart that you may be reluctant to ask. I wrote it to provide you with the type of guidance that will help you navigate this journey with some answers to questions I am commonly asked by new leaders. I wrote it so that you could learn from my decades of experience and avoid the pitfalls into which I fell, learn from the mistakes I've made, embrace the hard-earned wisdom that I've gained through experience. I wrote this book to be a resource to prepare you to lead God's church and people well.

Pastoral ministry is a lifelong calling—one that requires continual growth, wisdom, and adaptation. May this book serve as a faithful companion to you in that process, offering encouragement, insight, and practical guidance as you step boldly into the sacred responsibility of shepherding God's people. May it guide you during times of uncertainty and in critical points of decision as you lead His church. And may the Lord be with you as you lead the flock He has entrusted to your care.

CHAPTER 1

LEADERSHIP

Honoring the Past While Embracing Growth

When you first enter ministry, it is natural to follow the guidance of seasoned leaders, especially those who have shaped your faith. You may find yourself doing exactly what well-intentioned bishops told you to do, relying on their words without question. While their teachings are valuable and their wisdom deep, ministry today requires more than simply repeating what was handed down. You cannot rely solely on past instruction; you must continue to seek revelation and deeper understanding.

As a leader, you have a responsibility to build upon what you have learned, adding fresh insight while remaining anchored in foundational truths. In Apostolic Pentecostalism, the previous generations of leaders were directly connected to giants of the faith, men who stood at the forefront of the reemergence of classical Pentecostalism, shaping an entire movement. Their presence was so commanding that many of their sons in ministry became intimidated, relying completely on their teachings without pursuing revelation for themselves.

The people they pastored in that era were not as educated or spiritually astute as what you encounter today. Everything in the church once centered around the phrase, "Bishop said," and those leaders carried the same mindset into their ministries. The result was a failure to pursue additional revelation. Some believed that any new insight was dangerous, as if God had stopped speaking and that further understanding was unnecessary. The idea of gaining knowledge beyond what had already been taught was often viewed as sinful.

However, your challenge as a leader is to regain the spirit of revelation. You must not be afraid to pursue wisdom – not foolishness, but true insight. Leadership must never be stagnant. While you must stand firmly on the foundation laid before you, you cannot allow fear to hold you back from learning and growing. God is still speaking, and He expects leaders to listen.

The Need for Critical Thinking

Leaders must also embrace critical thinking in leadership. I recall the story of my pastor's friend, a fellow minister—a sincere, fine, and godly man—who once found himself in an unfortunate situation on a widely viewed television program. With the best of intentions but unaware of the context, he declared, "Every woman who wears pants is going to hell," not realizing that the host conducting the interview was herself wearing pants. He was operating under dead vision, clinging to rigid interpretations that had not been reconsidered in light of changing times. My pastor's wife, with grace and honesty, gently offered, "He can't help what was put in him." That statement raises an important question: Can you change what was put in you? The answer lies in learning how to think critically.

Being a critical thinker does not mean rejecting or discrediting the fathers of the faith. It does not mean discarding the truths they established. Rather, it means taking the wisdom they imparted and refining it for today's context. If you hold onto teachings without considering how they apply to the modern world, you risk becoming ineffective.

Many traditions that once dominated church culture were based on personal convictions rather than scriptural necessity. There was a time when women were told they could not expose their toes, leading to bishop board meetings debating whether open-toed shoes were permissible. I vividly remember an elder minister declaring to some women in the church, "We're not going another further. We already let you put your toes out!" These rigid standards extended to jewelry, makeup, and even education.

What many fail to recognize is that the pioneer fathers of the Apostolic faith were themselves revolutionary and revelatory in their time! They boldly broke away from Trinitarianism, forming an entirely different strand of church doctrine. Yet, the generations that followed them were afraid to cast vision for their own era. Many leaders were so concerned about being disloyal to the truths of their fathers that they refused to explore any form of refinement. However, you must understand that if Bishop Haywood or Bishop Hancock were still alive, they would not have resisted further modification and understanding. They were visionaries, and visionaries continue to evolve with time.

Passing the Torch Without Restriction

There are tenets of faith that you must uphold without compromise. My pastor once told me something that has remained at the core of my leadership philosophy: "My son should stand on my shoulders and see farther than what I saw." This statement captures the heart of spiritual succession. You must honor the wisdom of those before you while expanding your vision to meet the challenges of your own time.

When I speak to my spiritual sons and daughters, I make it clear that I do not expect them to become clones of me. My challenge to them is simple: Remain tethered to Apostolic tenets and principles, but apply them with fresh insight for today's world. As a leader, you must carry the spirit of the sons of Issachar, knowing the times and discerning how foundational truths should be applied to modern circumstances (1 Chronicles 12:32).

Even principles like modesty evolve over time. You must consider geography, culture, and social context when preaching from the pulpit. If your message does not resonate with the people within the environment where it is being delivered, it will fail to reach those whom it is meant for. Some preachers fear that adapting a message for today's audience is the same as diluting it, but that is not true. The word of God must remain pure and unadulterated. However, you must be equipped to deliver that word in a way that is effective within the culture you are called to serve without compromising the integrity of doctrine.

Adapting ministry to fit the times does not equate to disloyalty. Disloyalty would be rejecting the fathers entirely, dismissing them as ignorant, or refusing to recognize their contributions to the faith. That is not the goal. Your mandate as a leader is to stand on their shoulders, building upon the foundation they laid, continuing the legacy of faith, line upon line and precept upon precept. The question is not whether you will uphold their truths, it is whether you will lead effectively in your own time.

Leadership Success in the Kingdom

How will you as a pastoral leader know that you have been successful in the work to which God has called you? Success in the kingdom is about faithfully executing the ministry God has assigned, but not in isolation. Kingdom work is not about competition. In today's world, success should manifest not only as the advancement of your own ministry but greater cooperation among the body of Christ in all its various expressions, whether at the local church level or in the broader global church. We are stronger together, and the more we embrace that reality, the more effective we become.

To truly embody the kingdom, we must be broad-minded, which is sometimes difficult for church leaders and congregants alike. Many struggle with the idea that unity does not require uniformity. Everyone does not have to do the same thing the same way in order for us to be unified. The failure to grasp this principle is where leaders often fall short, including myself. I say this often because I do not claim to have it all figured out. The "my way or the highway" mentality is dangerous, and yet many of us, as leaders, unintentionally operate with that mindset.

The reality is that just because my approach is right does not mean someone else's approach is wrong. That is where broad-mindedness comes in. The kingdom is bigger than my understanding, my perspective, or my framework. If scripture declares that "Eye has not seen, nor ear heard, nor have entered into the heart of man the things which God has prepared for those who love Him" (1 Corinthians 2:9), then the kingdom is undeniably larger than any single person's vision of it. No individual has all the answers, nor does any ministry hold the sole blueprint for kingdom work.

Each of us has a role to play. I play my role, others play theirs, and together, we fulfill God's purpose. No one is required to preach exactly like I preach or lead exactly like I lead. Differences in approach do not delegitimize anyone's ministry; rather, they highlight the variety of assignments within the kingdom. Sometimes, we fall into the habit of measuring ourselves against someone else's assignment. Yet, there are people I will never reach because they were not meant for me to reach… but another pastor can.

What keeps us safe is adherence to the high principles of the church. We must ensure our assignments are aligned with God's foundational truths, while also recognizing that ministry does not always look the same across different contexts.

Beyond individual churches, we must see the greater need for one another. The world watches the church and often concludes, "You all are not together." If believers could move away from divisiveness and focus instead on complementing each other's strengths, the kingdom would advance in ways far beyond what we currently see.

CHAPTER 2

THE BUSINESS OF THE CHURCH

Operating the Church Like the Business It Is

One thing that is lacking in ministry preparation—and something I did not receive when I first got started in ministry—is proper training in the business of the church. While the church is an organism composed of its various parts, it must also function as a business due to societal demands. It must be operated with integrity, structured properly, and managed wisely.

I've seen a lot of pastors make critical mistakes in this area, starting with the establishment of the church. Securing the correct tax status for the organization is essential; establishing a 501(c)(3) with the IRS ensures the church complies with nonprofit regulations. Jesus said, "Render to Caesar the things that are Caesar's," (Matthew 22:21) reminding us that while we are in the world, but not of the world (John 17:16), we must still comply with worldly laws and legal regulations. There are certain legal responsibilities that we must fulfill, and pastors must take the time to understand them.

Church leaders must learn about taxes, finances, and proper administration, both in order to manage the church's resources and to handle their personal finances with integrity. Financial mismanagement can derail a ministry and even destroy a pastor. Ministry leaders must understand the significance of responsible stewardship to avoid pitfalls that could bring harm to their calling.

Pastors must also be administrators to some degree. Even if administration is not a personal strength, wisdom dictates that they surround themselves with skilled administrators whom they can trust and empower. No pastor is an expert in everything, which is why it is necessary to have others who fill in the gaps. Seeking legal advice and maintaining awareness of the delicate balance between church and government, as well as between church and society, is also critical. Understanding how to operate within that intersection is a skill that must be developed.

Handling Transparency and Accountability with Church Finances

The first priority in managing church finances is honesty. Financial integrity in ministry is essential because when people see that you are operating with honesty and transparency, they extend more trust to you. Members will support financial decisions when they know the finances are handled with care and openness. One of the most important aspects of financial integrity is following through on what you say. If a specific project was promised but could not be completed due to shifting priorities, it is critical to address that with the congregation honestly.

For example, there was a time when I planned to use funds for one project but later realized that another need was more urgent. Instead of moving forward without explanation, I returned to the congregation and asked for permission to redirect the funds. When they gave that permission, it ensured that I did not appear deceitful or as if I had asked for money under false pretenses. Transparency in financial decisions strengthens trust and eliminates unnecessary suspicion.

From the very beginning of ministry, every pastor should establish systematic financial integrity. Having a trained accountant and ensuring that church finances are reviewed yearly is an important step. Depending on the complexity of the ministry, this may range from a compilation to a full audit. Regardless of the church's size, financial integrity should be a priority from day one. It is never too early to implement systems that ensure accountability in managing the church's financial resources.

Church finances play a critical role in ministry impact. Provision is necessary to carry forth the vision, but proper management of that provision is just as vital. There must be systems in place to ensure that funds are handled responsibly. Providing an accounting to church members in a way that is clear and understandable also strengthens confidence in leadership, while the opposite is also true. Then, while financial reports should be available, members do not need to be overwhelmed with technical details. This level of financial oversight is best suited for the board and appointed officers.

One major warning for pastors is to avoid running church finances like a small family business. A poorly structured financial system breeds distrust. When finances are managed informally without checks and balances, it becomes difficult to maintain credibility. Establishing clear financial policies and leadership accountability ensures that resources are used effectively and in a way that honors both the congregation and the mission of the church.

Managing Church Growth and Financial Sustainability

As ministry grows, finances become more complex, and pastors must ensure they have the appropriate support in place. The more intricate the financial structure, the greater the need for trained individuals to help manage it. Staffing for financial oversight must be prioritized as funds increase and responsibilities expand.

I understand that not every pastor is naturally skilled at financial management, and that is something that must be acknowledged early. A wise leader surrounds themselves with people who understand how to work with money effectively. For example, my chief administrative officer is a trained accountant, and having that expertise within the leadership structure is invaluable. Pastors should seek individuals who are trustworthy, respect them as the leader, and possess the financial skills needed to maintain stability.

Some pastors hesitate to relinquish financial oversight, fearing that they will lose authority. It is true that whoever runs the money has significant influence, but pastors should not allow fear to keep them from bringing knowledgeable people into leadership positions. The key is accountability. Establishing a clear chain of oversight ensures that finances are managed properly while still allowing the pastor to remain informed and engaged.

One of the best financial decisions I made was recognizing that I needed someone to help ensure that spending remained balanced. While I tend to lean toward making quick financial decisions, I have trusted individuals who provide a necessary counterbalance. I may excitedly say, "Let's get it!" but they step in and say, "Wait a minute. Let's think about how this is going to affect us!" That kind of accountability ensures financial stability over the long term. Without trusted financial advisors, a church can wake up one morning and find itself completely depleted.

The larger the ministry becomes, the more help is required to manage finances effectively. However, I have witnessed how pride can become an obstacle to bringing on more help, particularly for pastors who have operated independently for many years. Early in my ministry, I assumed I had financial management under control. As the church expanded, I quickly realized that failing to seek assistance would lead to disaster. Effective financial management requires running the church with the same level of structure and oversight that would be applied in a business setting. Therefore, set pride, insecurities, and concerns about losing control aside and bring in the trained professionals to give the organization the financial systems and structures it needs to be sustainable.

Tools and Systems of Organization

I consider myself a techie, and technology plays a crucial role in keeping our church organized. We rely heavily on software that enhances our ability to structure, communicate, and create efficiently. One of the primary tools we use is Microsoft Office Suite, which provides a lot of essential functions necessary for church operations. We have also integrated Microsoft Teams and Outlook into our workflow, helping with streamlined communication and collaboration across leadership teams.

I encourage every church to invest in quality software that supports organization and efficiency. Currently, we are nudging our team toward embracing artificial intelligence as well. We use Copilot and are actively training leaders on how to implement AI tools to improve their work and ministry effectiveness. As technology continues to evolve, incorporating these resources helps us stay productive while maintaining clarity in leadership operations.

Keeping the Church Focused on Vision

Like any other business organization, a church must have a unique mission, which is a statement clearly explaining why it exists, and a vision, which is a clear picture of what the outcome will look like if it effectively accomplishes its mission. To receive vision, leaders must first seek clarity from God, discerning the specific assignment He has given for their church to fulfill. Then, this vision must be cast to the congregation with conviction, as it serves as the guiding force that calls people into deeper commitment to ministry and challenges them to give themselves to accomplishing something for the kingdom that is much bigger than them.

The vision must be constantly reinforced so that it remains central to the mission. Repetition is key. Churches should actively keep their mission and vision in front of their members, ensuring that it is articulated consistently and understood by all. A strategy such as repeating the mission and vision every Sunday may seem ritualistic, but it reinforces purpose and encourages collective buy-in. People can easily lose sight of why they serve, and regular reinforcement prevents distraction.

Realigning People to the Vision

Vision drift is noticeable within an organization, including the church. When members begin to lose focus, their participation wanes, and their engagement diminishes. They may shift their energy and resources toward matters that are secondary rather than remaining aligned with the core purpose of the church's vision. Leaders must remain vigilant, watching for signs that commitment is weakening. When these signs of vision drift begin to appear, it is time to get everyone refocused on the bigger picture again.

Bringing people back to the vision requires intentional effort. Leaders must preach it, teach it, and emphasize it in gatherings—particularly with those in leadership positions. The vision should be woven into every aspect of church communication and reaffirmed regularly.

Another practical step in re-aligning people is conducting periodic reviews of the church's activities. Leaders should ask whether the church's events and initiatives are truly advancing the mission or simply keeping them busy. It is possible to be highly active while missing the mark. Leadership retreats and structured meetings provide opportunities for reflection, allowing leaders to assess whether they are truly operating in alignment with God's direction.

A vision and mission statement must be more than a catchy phrase. While having memorable wording can be beneficial, the primary concern should be whether it carries spiritual weight. Vision should provide clear substance and definitive direction, pointing the church toward its God-ordained purpose. Ultimately, no church will thrive if it tries to be something it was never called to be – outside of what God has shown it would be through vision. Leaders must remain steadfast in their divine assignment, ensuring that their ministry remains faithful to its unique, vision-driven purpose rather than imitating other churches or trends.

CHAPTER 3

THE MINISTRY LEADER

The Leader's Call

From the time I was a young child, I always knew I was called to pastoral ministry. It may sound unusual, but as soon as I became conscious of church and what it was, there was an undeniable pull toward it. At the time, Bishop Samuel Nathan Hancock was pastoring our church. I watched him closely from the pews, studying his presence in the pulpit, the inflection of his voice, the way he ministered. Then I would come home and start "playing church," imitating everything I had seen.

If someone is looking for a mystical answer from me about how I knew I was called to preach and pastor, they would be disappointed. My calling wasn't confirmed through some grand supernatural event; it was a deep, enduring fascination that stayed with me. I knew in my spirit that this was where I was supposed to be. I once read about a Catholic nun who had been filled with the Spirit, and she described her certainty in her calling as knowing "in her knower." That's exactly how I felt. I felt a divine unction.

I was officially called to preach at 16 years old. Before that, I had a couple of dreams where I saw myself standing in the pulpit. Whether those dreams came from the Holy Spirit or from eating pork chops too late at night, I'm not sure, but I knew without a doubt! I embraced that pastoral ministry would be the ultimate expression of my calling. That certainty has been one of the greatest blessings of my life because, if I hadn't known for sure, I would have quit by now.

Being Sure of the Call

As you venture into ministry, be very sure of your calling. I would never advise someone to enter ministry unless they were certain of their calling. Even when you know, there will still be moments of challenge and doubt—seasons where you question yourself. Considering that ministry can be overwhelmingly hard when you know you're called, imagine how hard it would be if you were grappling with whether you were called or not in the middle of leading in such hardship. I would encourage anyone wrestling with their calling to stay before God in prayer until full confirmation comes.

Beyond personal prayer and conviction, affirmation of the call is crucial. This affirmation should also come from trusted spiritual leaders. Seek confirmation from those whom God has placed in your life as spiritual coverings. Let them know that you feel called and why you feel called and ask for their feedback on what they see. If you go to the right covering or mentor, they will tell you the truth. Scripture declares, "In the mouth of two or three witnesses let every word be established" (2 Corinthians 13:1). If God has truly called you, others will see the evidence of that calling. Ministry is not a journey to take alone—it requires the recognition and support of those who have been entrusted to guide and mentor you.

Developing a Culture of Honor for the Leader

As a leader, God says you are worthy not only of honor, but of double honor (1 Timothy 5:17). However, as you accept the call to pastor and enter into pastoral leadership, receiving the honor of the people should not be the primary goal of operating in the role. When you do what you are supposed to do as a pastor who is led and guided by the word of God, the honor will come. The foundation of honor in the church begins with teaching what God says about it. Scripture provides clear instruction on honoring one another, and this principle must be reinforced through consistent teaching. However, honor is not something that can be demanded—it must be cultivated.

Giving honor to whom honor is due, particularly you as a pastor, is essential. However, the process must be genuine. People do not give honor because they are forced to; they give it because they want to. The best way for a leader to cultivate a culture of honor is by fostering love and respect within the congregation. Love begets love, and honor naturally follows.

Young pastors should be careful not to prioritize honor over service. Seeking recognition prematurely can lead to misalignment in ministry priorities. The focus should always be on loving God and loving His people. Teach principles of honor, but emphasize them for the benefit of the congregation rather than for personal gain.

Defining Success in Your Ministry Assignment

Pastors often question what measures they should use to determine whether or not they are succeeding in ministry. I am very careful when defining success, especially in ministry. I believe success can become a trap for pastors if not understood correctly. Many today view success through the lens of numbers—how many people are in the congregation, how much money the church has, how much real estate has been acquired. While these things have their place, they are not the true measure of a successful ministry.

For me, success is fulfilling my assignment—carrying out the purpose that God has given me. It is about impacting the souls He has placed in my path and doing that work with excellence. Yes, a pastor ought to have members, but focusing on numbers alone can be discouraging. It is unrealistic to compare a pastor in a small town to one in a major metropolitan area, expecting both to have the same number of congregants. Even two pastors in the same city could have vastly different church sizes based on their assignment, and both could be successful.

The Bible affirms this principle in the parable of the talents Matthew 25:14-30). What matters is being productive within the sphere of your assignment and being satisfied with what God has entrusted to you. We must tread carefully when evaluating success, because at the end of the day, God is the final arbiter. Hearing Him say, "Well done,"

(Matthew 25:23) is the ultimate measure of a life well lived in ministry.

A pastor should be gathering people, rallying them, leading them. While there is no exact number to determine success, there must be some fruit. I remember a bishop who went seven years without baptizing a single person. Then, suddenly, his church exploded with growth. That same bishop once asked me about my church when I first came to Indianapolis as a senior pastor. I told him it was going slow. He responded, "That's good, that's good. You'll thank God for it when it begins to grow." His words stuck with me. Growth happens in God's timing. The Bible says, "The Lord added to the church daily" (Acts 2:47). Ministry success is not always immediate, but it is always in His hands.

Surrendering Plans and Preferences for God's Purpose

Leadership in ministry is built on submission to God's will. A pastor who refuses to yield risks leading their congregation astray. A shepherd cannot effectively guide the flock if they are not themselves listening to the voice of God. Attempting to direct ministry while disregarding divine instruction leads to uncertainty, confusion, and spiritual stagnation.

A pastor must walk with God rather than leaning solely on personal direction. Surrender is not simply a passive act—it is an intentional commitment to seeking His will, discerning His voice, and following His guidance. Without this posture, leaders will struggle to know how to counsel others, structure their church, or even determine what to preach. Spiritual leadership is not just a role—it is a calling that demands sensitivity to the Holy Spirit.

Pastors wrestling with surrender must cultivate consistency in God's presence. Remaining connected to Him requires more than casual devotion—it calls for fasting, consecration, and intentional moments of seeking His voice. Spiritual discipline strengthens surrender, making it easier to release personal plans in favor of divine direction.

Additionally, no pastor succeeds in isolation. Every spiritual leader needs mentors and overseers, individuals who have been given permission to speak into their lives and offer correction when necessary. Leadership is not meant to be a solitary journey, regardless of how long you operate in a pastoral or overseer role. Pastors must establish and actually utilize relationships with trusted voices who can help guide them through seasons of uncertainty.

The ability to surrender is not a sign of weakness—it is a hallmark of spiritual maturity. A leader who remains submitted to God's will finds strength in knowing that they do not have to carry the weight of ministry alone but that they have others who can help them bear it with them. When surrender is prioritized, direction becomes clear, purpose is fulfilled, and the church is led according to God's perfect plan.

Keeping Your Fire Burning

It's not a popular thing to say, but it is a reality: passion in ministry can wane. When it does, the solution is simple: return to the presence of God. Spiritual vitality requires constant, consistent, intentional pursuit of close, intimate fellowship with God. In the midst of the challenges and frustrations that leading ministry can bring, the absolute greatest way to sustain passion for ministry is to remain in God's presence. A pastor must consistently seek renewal through prayer, worship, and periods of sabbatical to avoid burnout. Reject the opinions of those who might tell you that you are weak or unspiritual because you need to take a break. Step away if necessary, take time to rest, and allow moments of renewal to restore your spiritual strength so you can return to serve God's people and His church with the energy and focus they deserve.

Another essential practice to keep one's spiritual fire burning is allowing yourself to be fed. Leaders must be careful not to isolate themselves in their own preaching, neglecting the wisdom found in others. Preachers who refuse to listen to other voices limit their growth. If the only sermons a pastor hears are their own, they are not receiving the nourishment necessary for continued effectiveness. Stay engaged with sound teaching. Listen to others, read widely, and remain open to fresh insights. Recognizing that learning is a lifelong process keeps ministry vibrant and impactful.

Ultimately, remember that you must acknowledge your own limitations. Do not be ashamed of them. No one is invincible, and ignoring personal exhaustion leads to spiritual depletion. Recognizing fallibility is essential for long-term effectiveness. When zeal fades, do not push forward blindly. Instead, pause, reflect, and allow God to refresh what has grown weary.

Keeping a Connection to Mentors

One of the dangers of leadership is believing that experience exempts a person from receiving wisdom from others. Many pastors and bishops may feel they have "graduated" beyond the need for instruction, but this mindset stunts growth. No matter how knowledgeable or skilled a leader is, they can still learn from those around them. I've been in ministry leading at a high level for decades, and I still regularly talk to, share with, and seek counsel from my mentors. You never get too old for it, but you can get too proud for it. Stay humble.

God often speaks through unexpected voices. Leaders must remain humble enough to receive insight, even from those who may seem less experienced or less trained. Spiritual sensitivity requires acknowledging that God can use anyone to deliver a timely word.

Pastors must also guard against pride. Ministry environments often elevate leaders, placing them in positions of honor and respect. While appreciation is valuable, it must not lead to arrogance. Be cautious of believing the hype that comes with status and recognition, ensuring that humility remains at the forefront of leadership. Your connection to mentors whom you respect and trust is a key part of ensuring that you are submitted to veteran spiritual leaders who can tell you when you are moving in the wrong direction, particularly in the areas of pride, arrogance, and entitlement.

The Leader's Preparation

It is always better to be prepared before stepping into pastoral leadership. Yet in our Pentecostal tradition, many are thrust into the role without adequate preparation. While nothing can replace the call and anointing of God, prayer and education are pivotal in augmenting what He has appointed a leader to do. However, many resist formal training, assuming that calling alone is sufficient.

I strongly encourage every young man and woman entering ministry to seek theological training early. It will equip them to minister more effectively, providing a deeper understanding of Scripture, theology, and church history. Unfortunately, many Pentecostals lack a historical perspective on the church, and this deficiency comes at a cost. Without an awareness of our heritage, we risk repeating mistakes and missing valuable insights that could strengthen our ministries.

Preparation is not just about formal education; it is also about time for reflection. Many emerging pastors have not had adequate space to seek God for vision and direction. Leadership requires intentional preparation in multiple areas, including preaching and teaching, but these are not a pastor's only responsibilities. Some of the most impactful work happens outside the pulpit, which is why relational training and understanding people are critical aspects of pastoral ministry. All of these aspects of preparation, including how to deal with people, should be introduced before pastoral leadership begins.

Few things are more damaging than a pastor who lacks people skills. It is a recipe for disaster. I have seen preachers who could preach the paint off the walls, yet their personality destroyed their church. They knew how to talk about God, but they did not know how to talk to people, and no matter how well a pastor communicates with God, if they cannot effectively communicate with people, their ministry will be hindered.

Pastors must recognize that their demeanor, personality, and interactions shape how people receive their message. A leader can be anointed, knowledgeable, and theologically sound, but if their personality alienates those they are called to serve, their impact is diminished. People are far less likely to listen to someone they do not like or trust. Pastors must understand that ministry is not only about delivering God's message; it is about ensuring that the hearts and ears of the hearers remain open to receiving it.

Staying Sensitive to the Leading of the Holy Spirit

Pastoral leaders must remain sensitive to the leading of the Holy Spirit, and cultivating sensitivity to the Spirit requires consistent practice. One of the most effective ways to do this is to develop a continual consciousness, or awareness of His presence. Ministers should not simply seek Him during designated spiritual moments but should remain aware of Him in conversation, in music, in interactions with others, and even in times of reflection. Asking whether God is speaking through a given moment strengthens the ability to recognize His voice.

When this awareness is cultivated, sensitivity to His presence becomes second nature. The Spirit will whisper direction, and ministers who actively listen will find themselves guided in ways that human reasoning alone cannot accomplish. Since God is omnipresent, leaders must always be watching, listening, and expecting His movement.

Sometimes, the best approach is to pause and ask, "Lord, what do you want to do next?" Learning how to let go of personal plans and allowing the Spirit full reign is critical. This applies even in moments of public ministry. Some of the most powerful moves of God happen when leaders step aside and let Him fill the room. At times, that may mean relinquishing a planned sermon in favor of divine intervention. More people can experience transformation in an unstructured encounter with God than through the most well-crafted sermon.

Including the Holy Spirit in Decision-Making

The pastoral leader should never make a decision about the Lord's church or His people independent of the Holy Spirit. The Holy Spirit should play a pivotal role in every decision a leader makes, because such decisions will have a direct or indirect impact on the people God has entrusted to the pastoral leader's care. While it is not always easy to remain fully dependent on Him, that should always be the goal.

Practically speaking, I know that sometimes, leaders are presented with a decision-making moment in which an answer is needed right now. Decision-making is often met with urgency, particularly in leadership settings where timelines and efficiency are prioritized. Many church leaders with corporate experience expect quick resolutions, but spiritual leadership requires a different approach. Rather than rushing into choices, I encourage pastoral leaders to seek confirmation from God. Even when logic points to a sound decision, allowing the Holy Spirit to affirm the direction ensures that it is the right one.

Scripture teaches, "Trust in the Lord with all your heart, And lean not on your own understanding; In all your ways acknowledge Him, And He shall direct your paths" (Proverbs 3:5-6). This principle must always fundamentally be woven into ministry leadership. There are seasons when human reasoning will fail to provide solutions, and God will intentionally allow uncertainty to linger to remind His people to rely on Him rather than the latest seminar or book.

Further, as a leader, you must teach the church how to follow the Holy Spirit through both instruction and example. Teaching biblical principles on His guidance is essential, but just as important is cultivating an environment where His presence thrives. When congregants see the Spirit moving among them, they begin to experience His leadership firsthand.

A sensitive leader models spiritual awareness for their congregation. The way a pastor engages with the Holy Spirit demonstrates to the people how they, too, should respond. Leaders should remain submitted to His direction in a way that makes the Spirit's presence unmistakable.

When individuals enter the church, they should encounter more than human effort. They should sense the divine presence filling the room. This is why the anointing is vital—not as something measured by volume or outward expression, but as the undeniable evidence of God's hand at work.

Discerning God's Will in Difficult Seasons

One of the most reliable ways to discern God's will in hard times is recognizing the peace He provides. Even in seasons of uncertainty, when a decision aligns with His purpose, there is an undeniable sense of peace that settles within the spirit. God does not leave His people without direction; He confirms His will through various means, often sending others to affirm and support what He is revealing.

The ability to discern God's will is strengthened through practice. The writer of Hebrews refers to "those who by reason of use have their senses exercised to discern both good and evil," (Hebrews 5:14). This suggests that the more you intentionally use your spiritual senses, the more sharpened they become. Discernment must be actively developed, ensuring that a leader does not grow disconnected from divine guidance.

Developing a Personal Study Routine

David declared, "...his delight is in the law of the LORD, and in His law he meditates day and night" (Psalm 1:2). I believe this verse reflects the posture every pastor should take toward study. Pastoral ministry demands daily preparation, whether for Bible study, morning worship, itinerant ministry, or other assignments. The rhythm of study must align with the constant movement of ministry.

On a personal level, I wish I could tell you I spend three to six hours in prayer daily like Bishop Tudor Bismark, but I cannot. Instead, I strive to maintain a prayerful spirit and dedicate time each day to study, though the exact structure varies. No two people are alike, and every minister must find a study rhythm that suits them. I am always pondering theological questions, and my designated study time fluctuates based on what I am wrestling with. Some days I focus entirely on sermon preparation, and other times, I take deep dives into theological concepts that challenge me.

My advice to every preacher is simple: do what works for you. Find your own spiritual rhythm. I am a night owl, which may not work for everyone. Some joke that I am a vampire because I tend to burn the candle at both ends—I stay up late and rise early. In my earlier years, I would study all night Saturday in preparation for Sunday, but now my process involves continual preparation throughout the week. I read, observe, and search for inspiration in everyday life. I do not get all my messages from books; I look for the message in the world around me.

I must also push back against some of my colleagues who insist on rigid preparation. As much as I strive for structured study, I am Pentecostal, and there are times when God shifts my message entirely at the last moment. There have been Sundays when I walked into the pulpit, looked at the congregation, and felt the burden of the moment, and God directed me toward something different than what I had planned.

A pastor must study with purpose while remaining open to divine inspiration. This is what makes the Pentecostal preacher unique; there is always an openness to being led by the Spirit. Yet even in study and preparation, the Spirit is leading, whispering that it is not the preparation itself but His movement that truly matters.

Know your rhythm. Set aside dedicated time – at least a couple of hours a day – but do not make the mistake of cloning someone else's formula. Every preacher is wired differently. I am a firm believer that you must be uniquely yourself so you can be the vessel God designed you to be.

Keeping Sermons Fresh and Relevant

Keeping sermons fresh requires listening to the voice of God, studying people, and staying aware of the times. Sermon preparation must extend beyond scripture alone. While the Bible is the foundation for what you preach effective ministry demands awareness of the world.

When preparing for a sermon, I do not limit my reading to theology or ministry books. I read across a broad spectrum. I am a news junkie, subscribing to multiple publications locally and internationally. I stay informed about events happening in the world because that is the ministry context; a preacher who is immersed only in scripture without understanding the cultural landscape cannot effectively connect the dots for their congregation.

Beyond reading, pastors must talk to people. You cannot live in a pastoral bubble. If you are not engaging with people, how will you discern their needs? Constant interaction ensures that you remain aware of the struggles, concerns, and desires of those you are called to serve.

I'm aware that some pastors insulate themselves for various reasons, often out of a fear of getting too close to worldly things or people and becoming contaminated by them. Thus, they separate themselves, choosing to take the "safe" route by isolating themselves to the church. However, I have found that staying in touch with your own humanity strengthens your preaching. You might be surprised at how often personal transparency resonates with an audience. Some of the most impactful moments in a Sunday service occur when a pastor acknowledges their struggles, and people suddenly realize they are not alone.

Thinking is also essential in order to keep sermons fresh and relevant. Be a thinker, not just about theology, but about life. Talk to the barista. Talk to the repairman and the security guard. Ask questions. Get to know people outside of the church, because if you have no interactions with them, you will lack any real context to minister to them.

Balancing Inspiration and Information

Rather than viewing inspiration and information as opposing forces that need to be balanced, approach them as complementary elements that must work together. Inspiration must have a foundation. If there is no depth of knowledge and preparation, the result is empty enthusiasm rather than transformative ministry. The inspiration of the Holy Spirit requires substance to work with. Without study, research, and learning, inspiration alone becomes mere perspiration, or intense effort without lasting impact.

Ministers should not compartmentalize inspiration and information. Instead, I encourage you to cultivate both intentionally. Read consistently and pray fervently. Dedicate time to theological study while also remaining sensitive to God's voice. Allow the Holy Spirit to shape how you articulate the word, ensuring that your sermons reflect both spiritual insight and intellectual depth.

Your personality and communication style also play a role in delivering the message effectively, but both must be developed through consistent spiritual and academic discipline. To be a well-rounded preacher, prioritize both preparation and spiritual sensitivity, making sure neither is neglected.

Speaking on Social & Justice Issues

Social issues must be addressed in your preaching, but they should always be discussed through the prism of scripture rather than personality. The goal is to speak truth without being drawn into partisan political rhetoric. I firmly believe that we live in an era where pastors must not remain silent on important issues occurring in the world around us. However, discernment is necessary in choosing when and how to speak and what to say.

Jesus exemplified this balance. He spoke truth to power, yet He also said, "Render to Caesar what is Caesar's and to God what is God's" (Matthew 22:21). He never aligned Himself with political factions, but He boldly confronted the moral and ethical failures of His time. Some refer to the Beatitudes (Matthew 5:3-12) as the constitution of the Bible, emphasizing that they lay out timeless principles that transcend political cycles.

Regardless of who is in power or which party wins an election, God's principles remain the same. Therefore, when society lacks compassion, for example, the church must call it out. If people are offended by biblical truth, that is something they must wrestle with before God. Speaking on justice, fairness, and righteousness does not require promoting political partisanship, it simply requires proclaiming: "Thus says the Lord."

The greatest biblical example of one advocating for justice is Jesus Himself. He was both an activist and an agent of change. Throughout His ministry, He engaged with marginalized communities, confronted corrupt leadership, and upheld the dignity of the oppressed. His teachings were not abstract ideals; they were direct calls to action.

John the Baptist also spoke against societal corruption. He called out leaders, challenged immoral practices, and refused to shy away from the truth, even when it cost him his life.

Several Old Testament prophets, including Amos and Jeremiah, were fearless in addressing societal ills. Amos spoke against economic injustice and exploitation, while Jeremiah rebuked the leaders of Israel for failing to uphold righteousness. These men understood that faith was not separate from the world's struggles. Rather, it was meant to illuminate them.

In my later years of ministry, I have come to recognize that speaking on justice is one of our greatest responsibilities as pastors. The church cannot afford to be silent in the face of oppression, inequality, or wrongdoing. Our task is not simply to preach salvation, but to uphold the values of the kingdom of God in a way that impacts society.

Evaluating Effectiveness as a Preacher

How will you evaluate your effectiveness as a preacher? If you ask a lot of preachers, they will tell you that you know you were effective from the crowd's response during the preaching moment. If they were on their feet, shouting their amens, crying, and pushing the preacher to keep going, that is often considered "effective preaching." However, from my perspective, effective preaching is ultimately measured by transformation, not mere emotion. In that same regard, congregational growth is not just about numbers; it is about lives being changed, people being inspired to live righteously, and believers walking closer with God. Thus, while engagement is important, it is not the sole indicator of effectiveness.

Avoid relying too heavily on emotional reactions from the congregation when assessing whether a sermon was impactful. Some messages are corrective, requiring boldness to speak the truth even when the people's response is subdued. A preacher must not fear delivering the hard word that God has placed on their heart.

An old Baptist minister once said, "The final amen is God's amen." That is the affirmation preachers should seek – not just applause from people, but alignment with God's truth. There is a fine line you will have to watch between engagement and entertainment. An effective minister must learn how to navigate both. The goal is to capture the people's attention without becoming performative, ensuring that the congregation receives a message that leads to genuine spiritual growth and transformation.

Preachers must focus on delivering truth with conviction while maintaining the ability to connect with their audience in meaningful ways. Striking this balance ensures that sermons are both compelling and transformative.

CHAPTER 4

GROWING, DISCIPLING & SHEPHERDING CONGREGANTS

Growing Spiritually Mature Members

One of the most critical responsibilities of a pastor is ensuring that their congregation is spiritually maturing. This process begins with what people are taught and how they are fed spiritually. Today, pastors must be intentional about regularly challenging their members, ensuring that their teaching and preaching include practical aspects of ethics. Too often, ethical instruction is overlooked.

While eschatology has its place, and prosperity teaching can be beneficial, neither should take precedence over the day-to-day realities of Christian living. Jesus' Sermon on the Mount in Matthew chapters five through seven addresses everyday ethics, providing guidance on how believers should live. If pastors are not mindful, they can end up preaching about the grand kingdom while neglecting the practical kingdom, the one people must walk in every single day.

Whatever a pastor's primary emphasis may be, they must always tether their teaching back to foundational truths. It is essential to remind believers that God gave us the Holy Spirit to direct and inform our walk in this life. The pastor must also internalize this truth themselves, staying mindful of their own spiritual discipline.

A structured discipleship program is necessary, especially for new believers entering the church. New members' classes provide an essential foundation, helping individuals begin their discipleship journey. There must be a formal component in the early days of a person's spiritual walk, ensuring that they receive solid grounding in biblical principles.

Beyond formal instruction, the responsibility falls on the pastor and their designated leaders to continue spiritual formation through ongoing teaching, preaching, and opportunities to serve. Discipleship is not limited to classroom settings; it is cultivated through life application, mentorship, and a continuous focus on spiritual growth. As pastors pour into others, they guide them toward a maturity that allows them to live out their faith beyond the church walls.

Advancing an Evangelism Strategy

Every church must have a structured approach to evangelism, ensuring that outreach efforts are intentional and effective. In our local church, we have an outreach and evangelism ministry that organizes formal campaigns and events, specifically designed to reach souls in a concerted manner. These structured efforts provide opportunities for targeted evangelism, ensuring that people outside the church are reached.

However, I have found that relying solely on these planned events leads to sporadic growth. Evangelism cannot be treated as an occasional effort; it must be a culture within the congregation. A thriving church does not just have an evangelism department; rather, evangelism must be embedded into the mindset of every believer. Every member should recognize that they have a role to play in spreading the gospel.

A successful strategy requires congregation-wide engagement at all times. The goal is to encourage individual members to see themselves as evangelists, understanding that evangelism is not just the responsibility of a designated ministry team but of everyone who carries the name of Christ.

Empowering Members to Witness

Empowering church members to witness begins with providing resources and teaching them how to share their faith effectively. This does not mean that the pastor alone must teach evangelism; rather, there must be mechanisms in place where trained leaders assist in educating the congregation on how to reach others.

Successful evangelism must be tailored to the community. It is easy for pastors to attend seminars offering evangelism strategies that have worked for churches with thousands of members. However, what is effective for a large metropolitan congregation may not translate well in a smaller community, and vice versa. Every church must discern what is best suited for their local demographic and the unique calling God has placed on them.

Evangelism is not a one-size-fits-all approach. You cannot take a big-city method into a small town and expect the same level of impact. Similarly, a small-town approach will not translate effectively into a major metropolitan area. Every local church is called to specific people, and pastors must tailor their outreach strategies to the primary constituents God has assigned to them.

An often-overlooked layer of evangelism is understanding who God has made your church to be and mastering how to reach the people within that assignment. Effective ministry begins with knowing your congregation, your city, and the unique challenges and opportunities that exist in your environment.

When evangelism is both structured and cultural, when formal outreach is combined with a congregation-wide commitment to personal witnessing, the result is consistent spiritual growth. A church does not expand simply because it has evangelistic events; it grows when its people live as evangelists every day.

Supporting Young People in Faith Formation

Our church invests in young people and in helping them develop a true, meaningful, intimate, and faith-filled relationship with God in a variety of ways, with a strong emphasis on community. We believe that creating a space where they can build relationships, engage in fellowship, and serve together is critical for faith development.

One of the primary ways we accomplish this is through KAM University, a structured program divided into segments for children, teens, and young adults. This weekly training provides both biblical instruction and life training, ensuring that young believers receive holistic development. We believe in striking a balance between spiritual formation and practical preparation, helping young people navigate both their faith journey and everyday life.

Additionally, we are engaged in a partnership with Fuller Theological Seminary (FTS) through a program called "10x10," which is working with PCAFI and other denominational bodies to reach young people more effectively. This initiative focuses on training youth leaders within local churches to be more impactful, equipping them with the tools needed to strengthen the next generation's faith. Our church helped FTS develop this program, and we actively participate in carrying it out. I would encourage other churches to explore partnerships like this, as they provide valuable resources for engaging young people in meaningful ways.

Staying Connected to Members' Real Needs

Pastors must stay connected to the real needs of their congregation by actively listening to both the people and the voice of God. The Holy Spirit plays an essential role in guiding pastors toward the specific needs of those they are called to serve. Not every person is assigned or called under a particular pastor. Some pastors are great for some people and simply don't work for others. Understanding that distinction allows leaders to remain focused on the flock entrusted to them and not be overly concerned about those who may not be a good match for the pastor-parishioner relationship.

Beyond spiritual discernment, personal interaction with the people is key. A pastor must never view themselves as superior to their congregation. Genuine engagement fosters trust and ensures that leaders remain grounded in the realities their members face. The Apostle Paul spoke about considering oneself (Galatians 6:1), a principle that reminds pastors to reflect on their own journey. Ministry leaders should never forget where they have been or where they currently stand in their spiritual walk. This awareness strengthens their ability to minister to the people they lead effectively and with compassion.

Training Others in Congregational Care

As the church grows, the senior pastor simply cannot care for everyone in the ministry on an individual basis, giving them personalized time, focus, and attention. This is where the next layer of leadership comes in, supporting and assisting the senior pastor with the work of caring for the congregation. However, the pastor cannot assume that other leaders organically know how to care for the people. Instead, the pastor must ensure these individuals are trained on how to properly care for the flock.

Teaching others how to care for the congregation begins with leading by example. Pastors must model genuine love, compassion, and service so that the expectation is clear. A ministry should embrace and emphasize these values so deeply that anyone resistant to them finds themselves uncomfortable in a leadership role. Caring for people is not an optional component of ministry, it is foundational.

A mentor once told me, "Sometimes you have to let the sheep walk on you." This means bearing the burdens of others with patience and grace. Members develop at different paces, and leaders must meet them where they are, providing guidance and support along the way. The role of a shepherd is to protect and nurture, ensuring that each person feels safe and covered.

Pastors often refer to themselves as a covering, but that title must be fully understood. Covering does not mean turning a blind eye to people's shortcomings, but it also does not mean abandoning people in their struggles. A true covering remains present in both the best and worst moments of a person's life. Shepherding requires both accountability and unwavering support, ensuring that members know they are valued even as they are challenged to grow. This is a lesson that pastors must not only understand but also communicate when training the next layer of leaders in congregational care.

CHAPTER 5

FAMILY MATTERS

Child Abuse

I once got a call from a tenured minister dealing with a child abuse situation, and it was clear that he had handled it completely wrong. He'd handled it so terribly wrong, in fact, that after the situation had been resolved, he and I shared a good chuckle about just how badly he'd handled it. He wasn't alone. Nearly all pastors learn through experience how to navigate such uncertain territory, making their own errors along the way. I've had to learn the hard way myself about how to handle such matters. When I became a pastor, no one prepped me for what to do in these types of circumstances. The legal responsibilities that come with pastoral leadership are often unclear, and with the stakes being so high, I wish someone had taken the time to lay them out for me from the beginning.

Every pastor must be fully aware of the psychological, spiritual, and legal implications of child abuse. There are laws governing these situations, and we are required to follow them. For example, I tell families in my church that if you come to me with an issue like child abuse and don't want the police involved, don't tell me about it. Why? Because by law, I have to report it to the police as soon as I learn of it. Failure to report such offenses can jeopardize the entire church operation. Pastors must understand both their moral responsibilities as spiritual leaders and their legal obligations under the law for issues like these.

Beyond the legalities, there is the issue of ministering to families affected by abuse. This requires a combination of pastoral care and professional support. Abuse cases demand wisdom, discernment, and a willingness to acknowledge when we need external assistance to deal with such serious matters.

Pastoral Discretion and Legal Awareness

Pastors must be especially mindful of how litigious today's world is. Legal awareness is no longer optional; it must be ingrained in how we lead, how we interact with parishioners, and even what we say from the pulpit.

In light of this, as a pastor or leader of a ministry, you absolutely cannot afford to speak carelessly. Understanding that a pastor might say a few things that, if interpreted wrongly, could have some serious consequences, some churches now delay live streams in order to give themselves time to mute things the masses should not hear. Taking it a step further, many will also edit sermon recordings to remove statements that could be problematic before they release them to the public for listening and/or viewing.

Sometimes, as pastors, we get caught up in the preaching moment. We might end up saying things that are not heretical or untrue, but they could be controversial and open us up for unnecessary criticism. Even if the words we preach are true, if they were spoken in the flesh, they have to go. They need to be censored or edited out of the message. Why? Because it's not just about truth; it's about wisdom. A word spoken in the wrong moment or without careful thought can have lasting consequences. Therefore, pastors must be thoughtful and willing to let their teams provide oversight and protection for the ministry.

Domestic Violence

Pastors must take a stand when it comes to domestic violence. I have heard leaders of past generations counsel victims to return to abusive situations, but this must never happen. I know of one story of a woman who backslid in her relationship with Christ. I heard a pastor remark to her that she would have been better off staying with a man and enduring abuse, because then, she wouldn't have backslidden. That kind of thinking is not only wrong, it is egregious pastoral malpractice!

Under no circumstance should a pastor advise anyone to remain in a situation of physical abuse. Sometimes, emotional abuse must also be weighed. I do not believe any man or woman should tolerate living under that kind of oppression, and it is great malpractice for a pastor to counsel anyone to stay in such a situation.

Infidelity

When faced with matters of people getting caught up in infidelity, and coming to me to ask what they should do about it, I often teasingly reference something Reverend Dodson said in one of his messages: "Repent, confess, and get rid of that mess!" There is nothing that God cannot forgive, but we must determine whether the person engaging in infidelity is simply remorseful or genuinely repenting. Sometimes, we fail to define the line between the two. How can you tell the difference? True repentance embraces the teachings of the Word of God and accepts the chastening of the Lord through the Holy Spirit. God forgives those who truly repent.

As a pastor, I advise you to always remember that you are not the Holy Ghost. Sometimes, without realizing it, we believe we can keep people from falling into sins like adultery, but the truth is, we cannot even keep ourselves! Only God can do that! Pastors are part of the equipping ministry; their role is to teach the saints how to tap into victory, allowing the Holy Spirit to lead and guide them.

We provide exposure to the Word, we teach accountability, and we walk people back to a place of victory. If someone comes to you as their pastor to confess, it means they want to be delivered from it and saved out of it. If they didn't, they wouldn't have come to you in the first place. Your job is to help them overcome—not to condemn them. We must provide a space of confidentiality that is also free from judgment.

I have observed over the years that many pastors have handled situations like this poorly, destroying families because the pastors lacked wisdom and discretion. One of the most important attributes of any pastor is the ability to exercise wisdom, and, frankly, some pastors lack common sense, and worse, lack a pastor's heart. Some operate more like butchers than shepherds, cutting people apart rather than guiding them with care. A surgeon carefully operates with precision, knowing when to cut and when to heal. A pastor must embody that same discernment.

If someone comes to you about being in an adulterous situation, I recommend that you minister to them with love and prayer, and then step back and give the Holy Spirit room to work. You cannot rush God; He doesn't just move on His own time when bringing blessings but when bringing deliverance, too. If you are dealing with sincere hearts, just give it time. Transformation will come.

I believe pastors take the sins and shortcomings of the people too personally, as if the people's struggles with sin are a blemish on the church's reputation as well as their own pastoral leadership. Pastors must stop worrying so much about their image and the church's reputation that they lose sight of what matters most: people being conformed to the image of Christ. Pastors, ministry is messy! You cannot lead and minister to the wounded without having bloody hands. Therefore, you must be strong enough to bear that burden and wise enough to endure the criticism that comes with it.

Divorce

I tell pastors that they can preach all they want to, but divorces will happen among couples in the church. You can establish all the marriage and relationship ministries, classes and events you want, but if you pastor for more than five minutes, you will encounter marriages that do not last.

I say again, there is no sin that God cannot forgive. While divorce should be rare in the church, it does happen, and the church must minister to those who are affected by it. As believers, we do not endorse divorce, but when it occurs, pastors have a responsibility to extend grace, healing, and reconciliation.

Every marriage is different, and every circumstance is unique. There is no one-size-fits-all response to how we as leaders should deal with guiding the affected parties through the grief and transition of divorce. This is one of the great gray areas of Scripture, one where room exists for deep discussion and debate. All that I will say is this: when the apostles encountered situations that were unclear in Scripture, they would say, "It seems good to us and the Holy Ghost" (Acts 15:28). With this, they were suggesting that they were relying not only on God's guidance through Scripture, but they were also using their judgment, discernment, and experience in their prayerful consideration of what decision to make about a matter. Many times, the answer is simply not clear. Not everything you will address as a pastor in ministry is black and white, and we must stop pretending otherwise.

Addiction

Addiction is a reality in the church, although many people conceal their struggles with it, afraid of judgment or rejection. While we in the church do not condone addiction, we must acknowledge that if a person continues coming to church, something within them is longing for salvation and deliverance. That alone is reason enough not to condemn or discard them. Instead, pastors must ask: How do we get them the help they need? How do we salvage people who are wrestling with bondage?

I say again, when it comes to situations like these, too many pastors, wanting to show others that they have a hard-line stance against sin and anything unholy, operate as butchers rather than surgeons. Instead of carefully addressing a person's wounds and walking them through healing, they cut them off completely. I wholeheartedly disagree with this method. This is not ministry!

When ministering to congregants struggling with addiction, the first step is to reassure them of the grace of God. They must know that grace is still available to them and that they have not fallen so far that redemption is impossible. Commend them to God's grace, reminding them that transformation is still within reach.

Pastors must also be conscious of their own backgrounds. Some pastors come from environments of addiction, giving them firsthand understanding, while others, like me, grew up in the church and have no experiential frame of reference for such struggles. Those of us who were raised in church must intentionally educate ourselves and seek training to grasp the reality of addiction. It may seem foreign or even ridiculous from the outside, but addiction is real, and people wrestle with things far beyond what we can personally understand if we have never experienced it ourselves. If we fail to develop empathy for struggles our people have that we have not faced, we will minister in ways that are ineffective and, at times, harmful.

Above all, it is important for you, as a pastor, to acknowledge that unless you have received some professional training in addiction counseling, you are not fully equipped to handle congregants' addiction issues alone. You must encourage them to seek professional help and to establish partnerships with professionals who can assist, so long as those partnerships do not cross boundaries that compromise spiritual guidance. The goal is to provide individuals with all the resources they need to achieve and maintain sobriety while creating a nonjudgmental, confidential, and spiritually enriching space for them to grow.

Additionally, pastors must be aware of legal boundaries, ethical considerations, and professional limitations when dealing with such serious matters. Even if congregants cannot have direct contact with a professional counselor, at the very least, pastors should recommend them to one. However, even while referring individuals to specialists, pastors must maintain a pastoral line of input so that their members remain spiritually connected as they pursue healing.

I know that there are those in the church who will insist that professional intervention is not needed to overcome the struggles of sin; prayer and a trip to the altar to tarry for a little while should get them healed of every struggle they face, including addiction. However, prayer alone for deliverance, while noble, is an incomplete strategy. Some struggles require both spiritual intervention and professional guidance. While it may be said with humor, the reality is that some demons need counseling—you can't simply "zap" everything out. All of it has its place.

There are moments when God delivers people instantly, but in reality, this rarely happens. If the pastors are honest, they will even tell you that they themselves have not been instantly delivered from all their struggles. Thus, before we as pastors assume that everyone's transformation should be immediate, we must acknowledge that even our own has taken time.

God moves in different ways and different timelines, and we must recognize the value of progressive holiness. Paul said, "I die daily" (1 Corinthians 15:31) reminding us that growth is ongoing. If people are sincerely working toward victory and deliverance through the grace of God, pastors must stand beside them, coaching them as they learn to appropriate the power of the Holy Spirit in their healing.

Many addictions are generational. While I do not use the term "generational curses," the reality is that certain struggles persist in families over generations. There may be genetic predispositions toward certain behaviors, though the root issue is always sin. Pastors must learn to take all of these factors into consideration when seeking to understand the sin struggles that their congregants face. Science and spirituality do not have to be enemies; rather, they can inform one another. Understanding that some battles may be linked to genetics does not justify them, but it does help pastors minister more effectively to those seeking total deliverance.

Regardless of the struggle congregants face, I always encourage pastors to remain open-minded enough to consider various possibilities of why the individual might be having these issues (like experiences and exposures of their past) while always keeping sight of the spiritual root. Ultimately, the key is to walk with individuals who are genuinely working toward freedom. Don't abandon the people you were called to shepherd. If the sin, struggle, or situation is drastic, perhaps the person may be removed from a very high profile leadership position in the church while they prayerfully work on their healing and deliverance, but that does not mean they should be removed from the church entirely. This is where our forefathers often made mistakes: they cast people aside when they should have sought to restore. Let's do better.

LGBTQ+ Issues

Ministering to individuals struggling with same-sex attraction requires wisdom, compassion, and biblical truth. One of the greatest lessons I've learned over the years is that you learn both what to do and what not to do by observing how the older fathers handled these situations. Often, their responses to LGBTQ+ issues in the church lacked grace and understanding. Today, it is our responsibility to ensure we do better.

I recall a situation where a young person confided in an elder, admitting their struggle with homosexuality. The pastor responded to this sincere confession and plea for help harshly, condemning them with words like, "You nasty, filthy, ungodly..." That kind of response is not ministry. It is not how we should deal with people who are battling something internally and seeking help. Paul instructs us to "speak the truth in love" (Ephesians 4:15). Even if a congregant is experiencing a struggle I do not personally identify with, I must approach ministering to them with love and humility, knowing that I, too, have my own battles.

The Hebrew writer tells us to "lay aside every weight and the sin that so easily besets us" (Hebrews 12:1). Everyone has a particular struggle – something that, if God does not help, they are prone to fall into. That includes you and me. Pastors must be generous in how they apply this understanding. Just because someone's struggle is different from yours does not make it any less real. It is still a battle, and it must be ministered to as such.

For years, my response to LGBTQ+ struggles was shaped by what older bishops had instilled in me. However, as I matured in ministry, I realized that some of my past approaches towards dealing with congregants who had these struggles did not reflect the love of God. I have preached things from the pulpit that I later regretted, because the Holy Spirit convicted me about how the things I said could have affected people with this struggle. When that happened, I humbled myself before my congregation and admitted, "I was wrong." Growth requires not only the ability to lead but also the willingness to acknowledge when change is necessary.

The truth is that if someone is struggling with same-sex attraction, God has help for them, just as He has help for all of us in whatever area we wrestle with. The key is that if they desire deliverance, God can keep them through their struggle and make them victorious.

I firmly believe that God can deliver someone from practicing homosexuality, but there are individuals who, despite overcoming the behavior, still do not experience attraction to the opposite sex. Pastors must recognize that some people will never marry. This is something we must learn to accept without forcing people into relationships that do not align with their personal convictions. I have had people confide in me, saying, "Pastor, I don't have a desire for a woman." We must be careful not to create a culture that pressures them into marriage simply because we believe everyone should end up in that institution. Some people, through their personal struggle, choose to remain unmarried as they continue to seek God for strength and deliverance in their struggles with same-sex attraction.

One of my old bishops once stated, "If you are 23, 24, 25 and unmarried, something is wrong with you! I *know* that you are out there sinning!" This kind of mindset contradicts itself. We declare that God is a keeper, and yet when He keeps someone in a place of celibacy, we assume He is not keeping them. We must allow people the space to walk in victory as singles without forcing them to project an image that makes others comfortable.

Pastors must also understand that there are things they know about their congregants' struggles that others in the church do not. The saints may speculate, but leaders, having access to more privileged information, can often see what is going on deeper beneath the surface. In light of the access we have to this private information on congregants, we must be careful about how we navigate these waters, ensuring that every soul is treated with the same grace and opportunity for redemption that Christ offers to all.

To be clear, neither I nor the church condones homosexuality, just as we do not condone fornication, adultery, or any other sin. However, the church must recognize that people struggle with different sins, and regardless of the sin or how detestable we consider it to be, we are called to help them through those struggles. If we are to walk in the maturity of Christ, we must approach these situations with wisdom, truth, and love. The church is not here to discard people but to minister to them and lead them into victory.

I will never preach a message that condones sin, but I do preach in the spirit of Paul—I speak the truth in love. There was a time when I spoke harshly, but now, I speak with the heart of Christ. I encourage you to adopt the same position as you lead the people He has entrusted to your covering and care.

CHAPTER 6

CONFLICT RESOLUTION AND CHURCH HURT

Recognizing and Addressing Conflict

Conflict is an inevitable reality in ministry. As long as the ministry exists, conflict will exist—and because it is one of the greatest threats to a ministry's stability, pastors must be equipped to handle it wisely. Conflict may occur externally between people, or internally within oneself. When dealing with members experiencing external conflict, pastors must be prepared to address disputes that can arise between individuals or within groups in order to bring everyone back to a place of peace, understanding, and unity. When dealing with congregants facing internal conflict, pastors must discern when spiritual guidance alone is insufficient versus when it is time to recommend professional counseling to resolve the conflict and bring the person back to a place of inner peace.

Dealing with conflict requires a great deal of wisdom. Often, the best resolution is unclear. In previous generations, pastors felt the need to have an answer for everything, even when they didn't. However, we must recognize that we are not experts on every issue. There comes a point when it is best to say, "This is beyond my capacity, so let me refer you to someone who is trained to help." Knowing when to make that transition is critical in pastoral leadership.

The Spiritual Reality of Conflict

Paul reminds us that "God is not the author of confusion" (1 Corinthians 14:33), meaning that conflict does not originate from Him. If conflict is not of God, then the opposite must be true; it stems from the enemy. Scripture declares, *"For we wrestle not against flesh and blood, but against principalities, against powers, against the rulers of the darkness of this world, against spiritual wickedness in high places"* (Ephesians 6:12). This reveals to us that discord is often rooted in deeper spiritual forces.

Conflict and division are ingrained in the sin nature of humanity. If Lucifer himself was able to persuade a third of the angelic host to rebel against God, we must recognize how deeply the roots of conflict and division run. This reality affects human relationships, even within the church. Satan's chief strategy is to sow discord, and pastors must be vigilant in countering it with constant reinforcement of unity and love.

At times, pastors fail to give proper attention to cultivating a sense of community and strengthening relationships within the church. However, stronger relationships decrease the likelihood that serious or severe conflict will occur among the people. Still, regardless of how close the community is, conflict will be inevitable. Since it is inevitable, our goal should not be conflict avoidance but resolution.

Some pastors treat church conflicts as unusual or problematic, forgetting that even the early church faced division. Not long after the baptism of the Holy Spirit, a dispute arose concerning the Grecian widows (Acts 6:1-7). If conflict existed among those fresh in their faith, we must acknowledge that our churches, which are composed of imperfect people, will experience it as well. Another example is Paul and Barnabas, who had such a strong disagreement that scripture says their contention was "not a little matter" (Acts 15:36-41). Yet later, Paul reconciled with Barnabas, proving that conflict does not have to mean permanent division.

A higher question pastors must ask is this: How do we remain in relationship despite disagreements? Learning how to navigate conflict while maintaining unity is an essential lesson for the church and a skill that pastors must learn to master as they lead.

Understanding Contrast vs. Conflict

One crucial distinction pastors must make is that contrast is not necessarily conflict. Sometimes disagreements stem from differences in perspective, approach, or personality rather than true opposition. What we label a conflict may simply be a contrast.

God grants wisdom to bring different perspectives together for the good of the ministry. Not everything labeled as conflict should be treated as such. Pastors must learn to discern whether an issue is truly divisive or merely an opportunity to merge contrasting viewpoints into a stronger, unified vision.

Managing Conflict Within the Church

When conflict arises in the church, I do not always handle it personally; I delegate much of it to my leaders. My lieutenants are trained to assess whether an issue requires my intervention or if they can resolve it independently.

I frequently remind them that their responsibility is to put out fires before they escalate. Many conflicts are petty and can be handled with wisdom and maturity. As you develop and train your leaders, you must help them to recognize their role as peacemakers within the congregation. Every leader must embrace the responsibility of being a firefighter in the church, keeping issues from spreading and maintaining stability within the ministry.

Church Hurt & the Perception of Being Overlooked

Church hurt is often expressed in phrases like, "My season at this church is up. I've been hurt too much here." When individuals come with these feelings, I let my lieutenants handle them whenever possible.

I've heard this statement at every level, from pastors to parishioners. Often, those who say it are simply seeking attention or reassurance. This is especially true of long-time members or leaders who feel displaced as new congregants and leaders begin to emerge within the congregation. These concerns are often rooted in subliminal jealousy and insecurity. God must grant pastors the wisdom to see this and reassure people discreetly, reinforcing their place in the community and strengthening their sense of belonging.

Pastors must always be perceptive—not just students of the Word, but students of *people*. Many times, church hurt is not a true grievance against the pastor or the church but a cry for connection and assurance. A simple gesture, like calling out someone's name in an acknowledgement during service, can make a world of difference. They think, "Oh, he knows I'm still here! He sees me. He values what I do." Even taking a moment to acknowledge the usher at the door, the sound technician who gets fussed at every other week, or the member who is rarely celebrated can eliminate much of the perceived hurt in the church.

Recognizing and valuing people is a simple yet powerful way to build unity. No one wants to be invisible. Everyone wants to be seen and reminded that they are seen and that they matter. You can accomplish this through simple yet intentional acts of acknowledgement. One of our longest-serving presiding bishops was a master at this. He would casually ask, "Man, where did you get those shoes?" or "Where did you get that suit?" These small moments created meaningful connections and helped people remember that their pastor saw them.

Pastors must cultivate an awareness of opportunities to create these moments, learning to grasp and act on them quickly and instinctively. Pastoral moments do not always have to come in the form of formal counseling sessions. Instead, they can be simple and often quick, personalized gestures of acknowledgment.

At the same time, pastors must teach a kingdom mindset within their churches so that members become more focused on purpose rather than personal validation. As people mature spiritually, their need for outward affirmation decreases, and their commitment to the mission of Christ strengthens.

Years ago, there was a video clip circulating in which a woman was harshly criticizing me about something I said while I was preaching. She was going on about the ill treatment of pastors toward people in the church. When I looked more closely at the clip, I realized that I recognized her. She was someone I had grown up with, slightly younger than me. I had learned many years ago, back when we were young, that both she and her sister had been sexually abused by her father. They were beautiful girls, and I remember the situation vividly. I also remember that when our pastor at the time found out about the situation, he put the father out of the church; that was the right thing to do. However, the pastor also put the girls out of the church, disfellowshipping them from the church because of the situation. These two innocent girls were devastated, and understandably so. Now, that was some *real* church hurt. I don't think they ever got over it. The fact that I saw this lady decades later criticizing me about something I'd said while preaching in my church was evidence of this. She had issues with preachers and issues with the church, and understanding her history with both, it didn't take much to understand why.

The watered-down version of "church hurt" people talk about today—being upset over the littlest things, like not being allowed to sing a solo—is nothing compared to that woman's hurt. While I could not condone the bitterness in her heart that was evident in the words she spoke on the video, I certainly understood it. Her greatest vulnerability was violated as a child because the church, which should have supported, protected and restored her, let her down. Because of that, anything resembling a sanctified preacher felt demonic to her, and in her mind, she was justified in feeling that way. I say all of this to say that the way that I processed this woman's hurt is how pastors must handle criticism—by stepping back and asking, "Where is this person coming from? What is the story behind their pain?" Process before you react to people's hurt and pain, because it always originates from somewhere.

CHAPTER 7

PASTORS' MATTERS

Attacks on the Pastor

I believe pastors talk too much. This might seem like a harsh statement about people who literally talk for a living, but many leaders find themselves in trouble because of it. A single slip-up can lead to chaos like an unwelcomed newspaper headline, a division in the congregation, the loss of a member. In today's world, a pastor can wake up and find themselves at the center of a viral controversy over one offhand remark. The best advice I can give is this: stay silent unless absolutely necessary. Like they say in testimony service, "You can't tell it all!" Stop talking so much.

Too often, pastors feel the urge to defend themselves against criticism, but most of the time, responding only makes matters worse. My pastor once told me something in my early years that I never forgot: "Whatever the pastor gives attention to becomes a big deal." Many times, pastors are their own worst enemy. At the first sign of opposition, they panic, react, and escalate the situation unnecessarily. I understand the frustration. No one likes feeling disrespected, and sometimes you genuinely are. However, pride can push pastors into responding to criticism through battles that should have been left alone. We preach about letting God fight for us, yet we rarely give Him the chance! What could have faded away quickly turns into a firestorm because we fed into it. Some leaders even bring their frustrations into the pulpit, unintentionally pulling the congregation into matters they should have ignored.

There are rare occasions when a response is warranted, but those moments are few. Most attacks are distractions, orchestrated to pull pastors away from their true assignment. Discerning when to address an issue and when to let it pass is crucial. If a situation does require attention, consulting with trusted spiritual covering ensures a response that is measured, godly, and beneficial. Without that counsel, it is easy to react emotionally and make things worse.

Handling Criticism

Criticism is inevitable in leadership, but not all criticism is destructive. Pastors must develop the discernment to recognize the difference between malicious attacks and constructive feedback. When approached with wisdom, criticism can serve as a tool for growth rather than a source of discouragement. Rather than dismissing criticism outright, take time to evaluate it. You do not have to respond to every critique, but you should always remain open to considering it. One of the greatest mistakes a pastor can make is assuming they are infallible. If leaders refuse correction, they risk alienating their congregation and losing the trust of the people they are called to serve.

I often advise pastors to "read the room," not only when preaching, but outside of the pulpit. Leaders must read the broader room of their church community, staying attuned to the concerns of those they serve. Surround yourself with trusted individuals, including leaders within the ministry who respect your role but are also willing to offer honest critique. These should be people who love both the ministry and you enough to say, "Pastor, you might want to consider this." If no one in your leadership circle feels comfortable offering you constructive feedback, or if you shut down conversations that challenge your perspective, you do yourself a great disservice. They will eventually go quiet on you, and while you will not have to deal with anyone questioning you, you also leave yourself vulnerable to being surrounded by people who will sit back and let you make mistakes without bringing potentially damaging outcomes to your attention.

It is my position that rather than avoiding critique, you should actively solicit it. Vulnerability in leadership fosters strength! Seek counsel from people you trust, and when necessary, make adjustments based on their insight. When someone offers honest feedback, resist the temptation to become defensive or frustrated. Recently, I asked my staff for input on whether we should take a different approach in some areas. Their responses provided valuable perspectives that ultimately led to improvements in how we engage with people.

I'm not saying that this approach will be easy, but I am saying that it is necessary. Many pastors struggle with sensitivity or even over-sensitivity to feedback that suggests they are anything less than ideal. While leadership requires confidence, it also demands humility. Openness to constructive critique ensures that decisions are made with wisdom rather than pride.

Handling Conflict Biblically

Conflict should always be addressed according to scripture, with reconciliation as the goal. Matthew 18:15-20 gives us the blueprint for how we should handle conflict with others and how we should advise our congregants to do the same. In 2 Corinthians 5:18-20, the apostle Paul speaks of how we have the ministry of reconciliation. We should never be okay with remaining in a state of conflict or discord with anyone, accepting that "This is just the way it's going to be, because we just don't see eye to eye." Instead, we should always strive to overcome offense and be reconnected in peace with our fellow brothers and sisters in Christ. Pastors should actively seek restoration and reconciliation within their congregation as well as in their personal interactions, and they should encourage those whom they lead to act likewise. Get over the stubbornness and pride and fight for reconciliation!

Further, I admonish you that when conflict arises, don't let it fester; resolve it quickly. Make this a part of the culture of your ministry. Allowing tensions to linger only deepens division. Few things grieve a pastor more than seeing members at odds with each other or experiencing conflict between themselves and their congregation.

Then, there are lessons specific to a pastor that must be learned. For example, you must remember your position. When conflict involves the leader directly, the pastor must refrain from lowering themselves into unnecessary disputes or getting caught in personal grievances. Thick skin is essential in ministry. Also, avoid using the pulpit to address personal conflicts. Some matters require private, one-on-one resolution rather than being aired before the entire congregation. Do not preach an entire sermon to vent frustration at a single individual or issue. Handle concerns privately, ensuring that leadership remains grounded in wisdom and dignity.

Processing Hard Questions from Church Members

People are people, and they will naturally have questions about a myriad of things regarding the pastor, the church, Christianity, and the like. Their questions will organically develop as they hear or observe things happening or when they are thinking things through and are unable to reconcile what they have seen, heard or experienced with their own values, beliefs and/or what Scripture says. If they are comfortable enough with their pastor or church leader, they will bring these questions to those whom they think will be able to answer them. Most of the time, they don't mean any harm in asking; they are just trying to understand by asking questions.

Pastors must avoid the instinct to become overly defensive when faced with difficult questions. The first place the pastor should start when being asked questions is asking himself or herself why they feel this is a "difficult" question. To the person asking it, it probably seems like a very natural, straightforward, and often innocent question to ask. Then, they should also ask themselves why this question makes them uncomfortable and why they instantly feel defensive when being asked such questions. I encourage pastors to remember that not every inquiry is a challenge to their authority, and perceiving every question as an attack will create unnecessary tension between leadership and the congregation.

That said, discernment is necessary. Some individuals may push boundaries or attempt to exert control over the church. If this is the motivation behind the question, a pastor should be able to sense it and respond to it wisely. A pastor must be able to identify when questions stem from genuine curiosity and when they are part of a larger attempt to disrupt leadership.

The reality is that church members today approach ministry differently than previous generations. Back in earlier times, church leadership went unquestioned; if a pastor or bishop spoke and ruled on something or held a certain position, that was the final word. The church accepted it and moved on, and anyone who disagreed did so silently rather than disrupting the unity that came with everyone accepting and adopting the leader's position on things. However, modern congregations are more educated and critical in their thinking. They are also bolder, so they are more prone to ask questions, seek clarity, and want reasoned responses. The old, "Because pastor said so," response doesn't work with them anymore.

Rather than dismissing inquiries, pastors should engage questions thoughtfully, offering wise, meaningful answers that provide understanding without causing division.

Further, they should encourage questions and be open when people ask for clarification or explanation about why things are done the way they are done in the church. A congregation should not feel that their questions make them adversaries to leadership. Strong pastoral leadership requires both authority and approachability, ensuring that members feel heard while still respecting the structure of the church.

Balancing Family and Ministry

Making sure the family stays intact while pursuing the call to lead God's people is a serious conversation that we need to have and continue to have in order to have healthy families while having healthy ministries. Pastors must guard against two extremes: neglecting their families for ministry or favoring their families to the detriment of the church. Neither is healthy, and finding the right balance is one of the greatest leadership challenges.

Inevitably, the pastor's family will have a unique perspective, expectation and preference of how things should be done because they are members of the pastor's family; meanwhile, the congregation may tend to have different perspectives, expectations and preferences. The reality is that neither a pastor's family nor the congregation is always right. Spiritual wisdom must be applied to both, and leaders must be prayerful in how they navigate the tensions between these two relationships. Finding that middle ground requires deep reflection, fairness, and consistency.

In many cases, both the pastor and the congregation expect the pastor's family to be as committed, involved and responsible for the church as the pastors themselves. When any member of the family, whether the spouse or the children, disappoint this expectation, the congregation can tend to shake their heads and judge both the pastor and the family members for what they see as a shortcoming or failure to walk responsibly in God's call. However, it is important to emphasize that while a pastor's family often shares in ministry responsibilities, they are not necessarily called to the pastoral office. It is important to make this distinction to prevent unnecessary pressure or unrealistic expectations from being placed on family members. To this end, watch how church members interact with your family, as some things, birthed out of congregants' misplaced expectations and pressures on your family members, may happen without your awareness. Also, observe how your family interacts with the congregation, ensuring that boundaries are maintained on both sides. If and when you see these boundaries being crossed, step in and provide reinforcement, reminding people of your expectations for how your family members should be treated.

I have observed many family issues over the years, from pastor-spouse relations to pastor-child dynamics in the church. First and foremost, I advise pastors to continually remind their congregations that their spouse is their spouse—not the church's. As a pastor, you must not assume that your spouse must serve as co-pastor or that your children must enter ministry simply because of their connection to you. If God organically calls them into ministry, embrace it, but do not force them into roles that are not their own. The church of Jesus Christ is not a family business. Honor the unique callings of your family members, especially your spouse, while allowing them the freedom to explore their own paths.

One of the most prevalent issues I have witnessed is how some pastors overcompensate for the church, allowing their own children to be vilified while protecting the children in the congregation. Other pastors go in the opposite direction, practicing blatant nepotism with their children, which breeds resentment among church members and weakens the ministry. Walking in the right balance is critical, because such issues can make or break a church. If handled poorly, the consequences may not even manifest until after the pastor is gone.

Then, there is the issue of pastors not making enough time for the family, which can lead to their spouse and children resenting the church and how much of it is required of their loved one. When you are pastoring, one of the most important aspects of maintaining balance is setting aside time for your family to simply enjoy being a family. Learn how to engage and when to disengage from ministry responsibilities. At home, be a husband. Be a father. Do not remain in "pastor mode" at all times.

I caution younger ministers to approach the issue of maintaining balance between the family and ministry intentionally, so they do not cause damage to the family—damage that can be challenging and costly to repair in the future. If I could go back to the days when I first began in ministry, I would have structured my life differently to better balance ministry and family. I would have walked the line more carefully while listening to the voice of God. If balance is not maintained, either the church or the family could suffer. Thus, I urge you to make intentional efforts to guard both, ensuring that neither is neglected in pursuit of the other.

Understanding & Avoiding Nepotism

Nepotism occurs when pastors favor their family members in an ungodly way, particularly in leadership decisions. For example, a pastor may advance their child to a leadership position that others in the church might be clearly more trained and qualified for; yet, they lock other candidates out and promote their offspring to a position they are unqualified for because they desire to see them have more power, influence or status in the church. This is damaging for both the church and the child. It is damaging for the church, because it shows that promotion is not based on merit, faithfulness, training, or qualification, but bloodline, which is an unfair criterion for leadership promotion. Then, it can be damaging to the child because they know they are unqualified but may feel the pressure to accept the ministry position solely because of their parent's position.

At the same time, pastors must be careful not to block their family members from stepping into legitimate callings. If God has truly anointed a child for ministry, that calling must be honored. However, it must be done with humility and grace. There must be no assumption of inheritance simply based on relationship to the pastor, and no one should be pushed into leadership prematurely.

That said, it is natural for pastors to want their children to succeed in ministry. Any father or mother would hope for their child to continue their legacy. However, Paul reminds us in 2 Timothy 2:5 that those who strive for mastery must do so lawfully. Leadership transitions must be approached with integrity, allowing spiritual confirmation rather than personal preference to guide the process. The congregation must perceive the pastor as a fair and impartial leader, committed to justice and the fear of the Lord. At the same time, I have seen pastors so determined to avoid favoritism that they became unjust toward their own families. It is a delicate balance, and neither the congregation nor the family will always fully understand the pressure the pastor is under when making leadership promotion decisions. This tension often leaves leaders feeling isolated, caught between responsibilities they cannot easily reconcile.

Finally, one of the most critical issues regarding family-ministry dynamics is the importance of pastors preparing both their families and their congregations for transitions. What will happen to the pastor's family when the pastor goes on to eternity? What's the succession plan? This is a difficult topic to discuss, but it is a conversation that must be had for the good of both the family and the ministry. The lack of pastors and churches having this specific conversation has led to chaos in the church more times than I can count.

The church is not personal property that automatically passes on to the family when the pastor goes to glory. In light of this, pastors must train both their loved ones and their church members to navigate succession wisely. Too often, ministries suffer painful leadership shifts because expectations were not properly set and plans and systems had not been put in place while the pastor was still alive. When transitions occur, the children of pastors frequently go from being fully included and preferred in the church to being treated as outsiders overnight. The pastor's spouse instantly goes from being the first lady to being an unemployed single mother trying to figure out how she will pay the bills and keep the house. This happens because church members also feel their own sense of ownership over the church, having poured into the ministry financially and emotionally. Their sense of ownership of the church leads them to feel entitled to choose another pastor and first lady for the ministry, allocating the resources to them while leaving the former pastor's family out in the cold. However, pastoral succession does not have to be ugly! Establishing, while the pastor is yet living, a succession plan for how the spouse and children of the pastor will be cared for—and for how long—will help the church to navigate these dynamics. It will ensure the transition will be handled in a just and spiritual way that honors and respects the former pastor, the investments and sacrifices of his family, and the pastor's legacy.

As a pastor, do not neglect your responsibility to put a succession plan in place. Even after a plan has been established, remember that it will require continued conversation and intentional training to ensure a peaceful transition after you are gone. I have seen churches experience healthy transitions, and I have seen churches fall apart due to poor handling of leadership succession.

Managing Stress

Whenever I am asked about how I manage stress as a pastoral leader, this is one of those areas where I have to say, "Do as I say and not as I do!" Too often, leaders present themselves as though they have uncovered the perfect formula for navigating stress, yet those who know them personally can see that they are not following all of the advice they give. This creates frustration for those looking up to seasoned ministers because it reinforces the illusion that other leaders have mastered something they cannot. The reality is that every pastor struggles with certain aspects of leadership. For me, it has been managing stress by scheduling time away for a break.

What I am learning now, in the later years of my ministry, is the importance of taking time for sabbaticals. Truthfully, I have only recently started making intentional efforts to slow down. Taking a designated day off each week has become a necessary practice, though it took years for me to listen to those advising me to do so. I finally decided to stop working on Mondays, a decision I now realize I should have made much sooner. It is important to step away from the intensity of ministry, even if just for a day, and enjoy something unrelated to church. Watch a baseball game. Sit on the back porch and do nothing. That downtime is essential for recharging, and when I return, I am a much better leader for those whom I lead.

When pastors neglect rest, they minister while tired and stressed, which diminishes their effectiveness. Fatigue leads to poor decisions, mistakes, and saying things that should not have been said. Taking intentional breaks is not laziness; it is wisdom! I advocate for scheduling weeks of concentrated rest throughout the year rather than waiting until exhaustion forces a break.

Many pastors operate under the misconception that their presence is necessary for ministry to function – that things will fall apart without them – but eventually, they come to realize that the work will survive without their presence. Ultimately, there will be proof that it will continue without them when the Lord calls them home and the church continues to go on existing. My question to leaders who feel that the church cannot function without them for a week-long break is, why is this the case? As a leader, why have they not trained, developed and deployed other leaders who could at least keep things running and not falling apart for a very short period of time when they needed to be absent? One of the truest tests of your effectiveness as a leader is whether people and systems have been put in place that allow the ministry to thrive in your absence as a pastor. For a pastor to operate with the belief that no one in the church can be made into a sufficiently capable leader to oversee the church in their absence, even temporarily, suggests that the pastor is operating with a hero complex. This hero complex in leaders makes them want to believe that everything depends on them, but in reality, holding onto that belief does a disservice to both the church and the individual. If the work dies with the leader, how effective was it?

As I grow older and become more aware of my own mortality, this question resonates with me more and more. It is only recently that I have fully realized how tired I am. Taking sabbaticals has been eye-opening, and I wish I had incorporated them earlier in my ministry. A young aspiring minister once approached me and said, "I want to be like you." I had to respond, "No, you don't want to be like *me*!" I say this because knowing what I know now, I would approach ministry differently if I had a chance to do it over again. One of the biggest things I would do, even as a younger pastor, is take regularly scheduled breaks. I have learned that sometimes I have to completely shut down to regain my sanity and peace. That means disconnecting from everything—turning off the phone, stepping away from people, and being alone with God. It is true that those in leadership must pour themselves fully into their ministry assignment, but it is also true that they must create seasons of rest. Without intentional breaks, burnout is inevitable.

Overcoming Burnout & Taking Sabbaticals

One of the greatest struggles pastors face is burnout. Many carry the weight of their churches as if the ministry itself depends solely on them, forgetting that they are not the church. Let me remind you of this: your last name is not Jesus Christ. He said in Matthew 16:18, "I will build My church." That means the responsibility for the church belongs to Him, because it is *His* church. Pastors must be faithful stewards of their ministries but must also release the burdens that only God is meant to carry. If God gets the glory for the church, then the challenges and struggles of the church also belong to Him.

Old Testament prophets often referred to their call as a "burden." Jonah, for instance, spoke of the burden of

Nineveh. Ministry is indeed a burden, but pastors must recognize that it is God who sustains them as they carry the burden. Too often, especially in Pentecostal and Apostolic circles, pastors take on an unhealthy level of responsibility, carrying weight they were never meant to hold. This leads to exhaustion, frustration, and eventually spiritual depletion and burnout.

As I have said, pastors must learn to step away when necessary, allowing space for renewal. Winding down does not mean neglecting the church; it means acknowledging that the church belongs to God. A leader must intentionally create moments of rest, sometimes sitting in the presence of the Lord without an agenda. There is value in simply being still.

I will never forget one of my most freeing experiences. We were in the middle of a major building project, and my pastoral staff noticed the stress weighing on me. Without asking, they made arrangements for me to leave—alone. No spouse, no children, no attendants… just me. They planned out the trip for me to go spend time at a timeshare one of them owned. They simply said, "Bishop, no questions. You are going." Initially, I was caught off guard, but I appreciated the fact that they saw the weight of the burden I was carrying. It amazed me that my leaders recognized my stress level even before I did. They saw the toll it was taking on me and shut me down for my own well-being—to preserve me as their leader. So, I packed my bags and went.

After landing at the airport and arriving at the timeshare, I remember what happened like it was yesterday. I literally walked in, sat my luggage down, opened the blinds, and looked out at the Florida sunshine. Then, I sat. For hours, I did nothing. I did not think. I did not pray. I did not make requests. It was one of the most liberating moments I have ever experienced. I had not realized how deeply exhausted I was until I finally paused. Sometimes, doing nothing is the best thing a pastor can do, not just for themselves, but for the church.

It is a reality that we must face: pastors need alone time. Much emphasis is placed on family time, but too little is said about personal time alone and the renewal it brings. Sometimes even pastors' spouses need individual space to unwind and allow God to minister to them. Thus, sabbaticals are vital. Not every pastor can afford to step away for months at a time, but every leader must create opportunities for rest. If the plan is to take a four-week break and the time can't be taken at one time, schedule the time as individual weeks throughout the year. Then, when you get away, don't spend your mental time and energy thinking about what's happening to the church. Christ will take care of His church in your absence. The only way to truly embrace renewal and enjoy your break is to recognize that this is not your church, it is God's, and let both your mind and body rest.

Before you keep going nonstop and work yourself into burnout and an untimely death, remember this: no pastor is indispensable. The church will continue beyond the tenure of any leader. One day, there will be another name on the sign, another person in the office, another individual sitting in the chair. One of my most vivid memories was when I was a child, and I was watching the coverage of the assassination of President John F. Kennedy. I'll never forget what I saw: Lyndon B. Johnson was sworn in as the new president while the slain President Kennedy's body lay in a coffin behind him, still on the plane. Life continued. The world went on without JFK, and the church will go on without you. So, pastor, take a break! Pastoring is a privilege, but pastors must never assume the church will collapse without them. Ministry belongs to God, and in His wisdom, He sustains it beyond the lifetime of any single leader.

Seeking Counseling and Support

Whenever things become too much for me to handle alone, I seek counsel and support. I do it all the time. That is why I have a pastor. When the pressures of ministry become overwhelming, I recognize the need for outside counsel, help, support, and encouragement. There have been moments when the emotional weight of leadership felt so heavy that I wrestled with elements of depression. I recall that one of the most challenging seasons of ministry like this was during the COVID pandemic. The pace, the isolation, and the uncertainty made it especially difficult, and I would not have been able to get through it without the voice and counsel of my mentors.

I have always leaned on my pastor for counsel—first Bishop Smith before he passed, and now Bishop Nelson. While neither of them are professional therapists, I can say that I have been able to tell them anything. I can share my heart with no fear of shame, judgment or condemnation; very little about my life has been held back from them. They have been my "therapists without papers," and their role in my life has been invaluable.

I encourage every pastor to have the same support system in place. Even though you are a pastor, you should have your own pastor—a covering that not only watches your ministry and holds you accountable but who also serves as a safe place and a place for wise counsel. At a minimum, every leader needs one place of catharsis—a space where they can be completely honest without fear of judgment. You'll need it for your mental health and wholeness. Having these safe, secure spaces to receive counsel is a large part of what allows a pastor to continue serving without becoming entirely overwhelmed by the pressures of ministry. However, it should be said that when you still feel overwhelmed after speaking to your pastor and circle of mentors and counselors, and your feelings of stress and depression become debilitating in any way, you should seek professional help. I strongly advocate for therapy, and I believe pastors should be willing to consult trained professionals when needed.

Protecting Your Heart in Ministry

Although many pastors and leaders try to protect their heart from those who might hurt them, whether intentionally or unintentionally, I do not believe that you can truly protect your heart from the people you serve, because as their shepherd, your heart should be open to them. The best thing you can do is ask God to guard your heart and then step aside, allowing Him to do the work. Ministry requires vulnerability. Just as a man and woman cannot truly love one another unless they open themselves up to one another, the same principle applies to pastoring – a pastor cannot truly love his sheep if his heart is not open to them.

If you are too focused on self-preservation, you may never be able to express the love of God to the congregation the way you ought to.

If you will be a pastor, prepare to have your heart broken—it is an inevitable reality of ministry. The good news is that God heals broken hearts. Thus, instead of trying to shield yourself from the inevitable, ask the Lord to give you the ability to navigate those painful moments and endure them with grace.

Setting Boundaries in Pastoral Relationships

Every pastor must establish boundaries between himself and those whom he leads in order to maintain the proper levels of respect, structure, and order necessary for effective leadership and church functioning. Boundaries in pastoral relationships begin with an awareness of roles. Even if a close friend is a member of the church, they must always recognize that you are their pastor first and relate to you as such. Pastors must be selective about who they allow into their close circle, ensuring that relationships remain both supportive and respectful of pastoral authority. If people in the circle cannot respect the boundaries you put into place delineating how they should—and should not—relate to you, especially publicly, it might be best to place them back outside of the circle.

Maintaining the boundary between pastor and congregant is important, because even if the congregant is a friend, there will be moments when it is necessary for you to operate as pastor and correct them. If they have properly maintained the boundary, they will receive what you say to them as their pastor and not dismiss your words of rebuke, reproof, and correction because of their proximity to you. Even close friendships must remain open to rebuke and accountability from the pastor, ensuring that leadership responsibilities are not compromised, because the wellbeing of the ministry is much greater than the friendship.

One of the mistakes many young pastors make is becoming too familiar with their congregation. While I am not advising pastors to avoid personal interactions, I do caution them to maintain a level of professional and spiritual distinction between themselves and their congregants. Members should not see their pastor engaging in any and every behavior—even if the behaviors are not sinful. There must be intentional boundaries around how much is shared publicly, because people who are looking for reasons to accuse and discredit the pastor can choose to read into or misinterpret anything he shares. Discretion of pastors should particularly be observed when it comes to sharing about their personal lives on social media. While transparency about their lifestyles can build connection with people, oversharing can diminish the sanctity of the pastoral office. You and your family may enjoy taking pictures of moments in your life, but not everything needs to be shared with the congregation. Some aspects of family life should remain private.

Many young leaders have lost this sense of balance. Social media, in particular, has led pastors to speak too freely, comment on everything, and expose too much. Every action and statement can be memorialized, and words spoken in the moment can have lasting consequences. Leaders must remain intentional about seeking the Holy Spirit's guidance in how they communicate and present themselves.

Healthy boundaries between pastors and their congregants are necessary for maintaining a healthy culture of respect, admiration and leadership authority in the church. In attempting to be approachable, some pastors become too common and familiar with congregants, causing them to lose the reverence and mystery associated with their position. They try to be "just one of the guys" or "a regular person like anyone else," but because of the call, they are not. God called them to lead the sheep as a shepherd; there is a difference—and it should be respected. The pastor, because of his call and his role, is to be respected, revered, honored and held in higher esteem. A congregation should not fear its leader, but there should be a level of honor that fosters their respect of their pastor and his authority. As a result of their esteem and honor for their pastor, members should instinctively recognize certain conversations or actions as inappropriate around their pastor. However, they will only operate with such a consciousness if boundaries are set and enforced.

Maintaining Respectable Character

Character is something that God preserves. However, as a pastor, you are also responsible for carrying yourself in a way that helps keep you above reproach. This is ultimately a God-ordained process. I came up in an era of ministry in which preachers were considered untouchable, but I believe that such a model hinders pastors from being truly effective. There must be a balance. A leader must be touchable but not common. The difference between the two is how you carry yourself. You must maintain respectability while also allowing people to see and experience your humanity.

Some leaders present themselves in a robotic fashion, creating emotional distance between themselves and their congregations. Yet, if people do not feel a connection with you, the depth of their followership will be shallow. People must see their pastor as a man or woman of God, but they must also be able to relate to them beyond the pulpit. If you are a pastor having challenges in this area, pray that God will show you how to foster connection with your congregants without becoming too common. There is no hard, fast, or black-and-white answer for how to strike this balance. I believe that only God can show pastors how to balance authority with accessibility, and if you sincerely seek Him for how to do this, He will help you.

Battling Addiction

Pastors are human, not superhuman. They wrestle with sin the same way everyone else does and are not immune from attacks of the enemy. Thus, things like addiction happen – yes, even among pastors. If you are a pastor who finds yourself struggling with addiction, you must not be afraid to seek help. However, wisdom is required in choosing where to seek that help. As a pastor, you must surround yourself with trusted individuals who genuinely have your best interests at heart. At the same time, discretion is necessary. Not everyone can be trusted with a leader's vulnerability. Despite the need for caution, no pastor can face addiction alone; they must have accountability and support to navigate their struggle without being destroyed in the process.

If pastors establish strong accountability with their own pastor and trusted mentors from the beginning, it greatly reduces the likelihood that addiction will overwhelm them. However, if they do find themselves in a season of struggle, having accountability ensures that someone is there to help them get through that season and back to sanity. Accountability in leadership is not just about preventing failure; it is about ensuring restoration when mistakes happen. Pastors must have relationships that provide both preventive safeguards and pathways to recovery. Seeking help early and walking through the process wisely can make the difference between falling completely and finding the strength to get back up again. As with any serious issue like addiction, I urge you to seek the attention of a trained professional to support you in overcoming your addiction and maintaining sobriety.

Setting Up Accountability

I do not believe that there ever should be such a thing as a pastor who does not have a pastor. In fact, accountability *begins* with the principle that every pastor must have a pastor, not just as a figurehead or a formality, but as someone to whom they are submitted—someone they listen to and whose counsel they don't just seek, but follow. Beyond that, pastors must surround themselves with mentors and colleagues whom they respect and with whom they share mutual accountability. There must be people in ministry who can speak freely without pulling punches, ensuring honest and direct dialogue.

I've always said that an isolated pastor is a dangerous pastor! A leader who operates in a vacuum and has no trusted friendships outside their congregation runs the risk of making unchecked decisions and falling into personal and spiritual pitfalls. You may say, "I don't need any outside sources to advise me. I have people in my church who I bounce things off of and who give me wise counsel." That seems nice, but you must remember that your members, while supportive, often tell you what you *want* to hear, because you are their leader. They don't want to disappoint, offend or discourage you, so they can tend to not tell you the raw, unfiltered truth – a truth that is needed so that you don't destroy yourself or sabotage your own leadership.

That is why you need real friends – long-term connections with people who know you beyond your title and who can challenge you with unfiltered truth when necessary. You need voices of authority that you have intentionally empowered to speak into your life. However, you can't just listen to them speak; you must be willing to change the way you think based on the feedback they give you. As a pastor, submission is required. Just as you expect others to be accountable to you and your leadership, you must remain accountable as well. A leader who refuses to be accountable to another leader sets themselves up for disaster. I have seen it happen far too many times—and it never ends well.

The congregation should also know that their pastor has someone holding them accountable. A church cannot be expected to walk in accountability if its pastor does not lead by example. The pastor should be transparent about who holds them accountable, sharing this with the congregants. This level of transparency strengthens the people's trust in their pastor's leadership. Knowing their pastor is accountable to someone who speaks truthfully into their life about their actions and decisions gives people a greater sense of confidence that they are in good hands.

Recovering and Responding After Making Mistakes

No pastor is infallible, so inevitably, every pastor will make mistakes. However, there is a way to respond to and recover from mistakes in order to minimize the damage it can have on the ministry. It's pretty simple: a pastor recovers by being honest. If a mistake is made, it should be acknowledged rather than ignored. This is also true retroactively; I have gone back to my congregation and admitted that there are things I would do differently now than I did as a younger pastor. Owning past decisions demonstrates humility and wisdom.

The worst thing you can do when you make a mistake is deny that you made the mistake! You would be surprised at how forgiving people can be when you are up front and honest with them about the error, even if you don't give them all of the details. The admission of the error and apology are often enough. They know that you are human and that you make mistakes like everyone else. It is the attempt to cover up mistakes that leads to broken trust. If a leader attempts to conceal an error and the congregation later discovers it, the resulting loss of confidence is far more damaging than the initial mistake itself. Transparency breeds trust, and trust is essential for longevity in ministry.

At the same time, not every aspect of a pastor's life is meant for public consumption. There are certain pastoral decisions that should be kept between a pastor and their own covering. A pastor's personal struggles and challenges do not always need to be shared publicly, just as congregants aren't expected to share their personal struggles publicly. Sanctification issues that people are struggling with and believing God for deliverance and salvation from can usually be kept between them and the Holy Spirit. The same is true for pastors. Even though pastors live in the spotlight, not every part of their life is meant to be exposed.

Ultimately, balance is required. Pastors must be honest when necessary, admit their mistakes when appropriate, and maintain discretion in areas that should remain private. Learning when to be transparent and when to seek confidential counsel is one of the greatest tools for longevity and wisdom in ministry, so learn to master it early.

CHAPTER 8

CHURCH MATTERS

Transitioning Members Out of and Into the Congregation

Every pastor will face moments where transitions in their congregation occur—when members leave and move on to other things. Knowing when it is time for someone to go and how to release them without bitterness is one of the most difficult aspects of ministry leadership. As pastors, we often identify our personhood too closely with our church, making rejection of our pastoral leadership feel like rejection of who we are personally. It is difficult not to internalize this pain. But how do pastors guard their hearts from becoming bitter after repeated heartbreak?

Bishop James A. Johnson once spoke a prophetic word that unwittingly prepared Bishop Nelson for this reality: "Ministry wounds are inevitable, but they must not consume us. Learning how to accept departures without resentment is an essential skill."

Additionally, pastors must be wise in how they receive new members from other churches. One principle I always share with pastors is this: listen to how newcomers speak about their previous pastor. Nine times out of ten, they will eventually speak the same way about you. A member who dishonors their former shepherd will likely dishonor their new one in time. Biblical precedent reinforces this truth. When David encountered the man who claimed to have killed Saul, David did not celebrate him—he executed him! This principle reminds pastors to be cautious in handling individuals who shift from one congregation to another, ensuring that transitions are made with integrity, wisdom, and discernment.

Healthy Church Growth

Church growth encompasses two dimensions: growing those already in the church and bringing in new people from the community. The danger is in emphasizing one while neglecting the other. Some churches focus entirely on internal community building, which can result in a closed congregation. Others focus exclusively on numerical expansion, chasing growth metrics while failing to nurture individuals. Healthy growth requires both outreach and spiritual development, ensuring that new members feel connected while existing members continue to thrive.

The first key to healthy church growth is avoiding the trap of the numbers game. Growth is important, but it cannot be measured solely by the number of conversions, baptisms, or people being filled with the Spirit. While these moments are significant, they do not offer a full picture of spiritual development. At the same time, pastors must not fall into complacency, accepting stagnation as normal. Growth must be both measurable and meaningful.

One aspect of healthy church growth that often gets overlooked is winning what is called the "back door war." For example, a church can report impressive baptism numbers, but the real question is whether those new members are still engaged a few weeks later. Every pastor must be honest with themselves about retention by asking some critical questions related to church growth. Where are the people who joined recently? Have they remained, or have they quietly slipped away, and why?

Member assimilation is key to lasting growth. True discipleship involves not only introducing people to faith but helping them root themselves in the church. A healthy church is one where members build strong relationships, actively participate in ministry, and integrate into the life of the congregation. These elements of connection, involvement, and stability are just as important as numerical growth.

When it comes to measuring church growth by numbers, I agree that setting goals for church growth is perfectly valid, as these metrics can provide direction for leadership. However, all growth must be understood within the framework, based on 1 Corinthians 3:6, that it is God who ultimately determines the increase. Pastors should seek to be productive within their assigned sphere and trust that the timing and expansion of their ministry remain in His hands.

Balancing Growth with Intimacy and Connection

Church growth must be intentional, but it must also foster community and intimacy. Without this emphasis, churches can become mere machines – efficient but disconnected. Growth that is purely structural often results in members who never develop deep roots. There must be clear mechanisms for building community within the church. Programs, events, and activities should not exist solely for celebration or ministry functions but also for the purpose of fellowship. A church must provide space for people to connect beyond formal worship settings.

I have always prioritized fellowship, even though I have never found small groups to be particularly effective in my ministry. It is clear that they work in some contexts, but in other contexts, they do not. A prominent leader once suggested that small groups may function differently based on socioeconomic or cultural factors, which is a possibility worth considering. Regardless of the approach, whether through structures such as small groups or not, church leaders must focus on connection and relationships, ensuring that ministry extends beyond tasks into helping people to develop meaningful relationships.

For example, one way my ministry has found to build connection is through ushers and hospitality teams. These roles should not merely direct people to their seats but should also facilitate engagement and follow-up. When structured correctly, they provide a critical touchpoint for newcomers, helping them navigate their early days in the church while integrating them into the broader community. However, this is something that works for me in my ministry context; every church must identify what works for them to help people build connection. One mistake pastors make is adopting a cookie-cutter approach, believing that what has worked elsewhere will automatically work in their church.

The personality of the church matters, and the intimacy of relationships must be cultivated in a way that aligns with the existing environment.

A church's ability to maintain intimacy is also influenced by the personality and interaction of the pastor. Leaders must find ways to be personable without imitating someone else's style. Congregants must sense that their pastor's concern is genuine and sincere, not performed out of obligation. As a church grows, pastors should make time for personal moments of connection. This may mean staying a few minutes after service to shake hands, greet people, and hold short conversations. It may also mean crafting sermons in such a way that allows members to feel connected to the leader personally. Every pastor must find their own way to foster connection, understanding how critical it is to the health of the church.

Overcoming Church Growth Obstacles

One of the biggest obstacles to church growth is trying to be like other pastors or other churches. Many pastors struggle with this, attempting to imitate larger or more well-known ministries without considering whether those strategies are suited for their own church. Authenticity is key! Church growth must flow from an approach that aligns with the pastor's identity, the ministry's context, and the people the church is called to reach.

Another major church growth challenge is that sometimes, pastors remain too wedded to past traditions when attempting to grow a church. They often fail to recognize when times have changed, and change can unfold right in front of them—often without notice. In fact, a congregation's preferences, needs, and expectations can slowly shift while leadership remains stuck in outdated methods of church growth and connection, resulting in a lack of sustained church growth. Pastoral resistance to changing or adapting strategies and techniques that can grow a church can be either intentional or unintentional. Some pastors deliberately hold fast to old ways, unwilling to adjust. Others fail to recognize the need for adaptation simply because they have not paid attention to shifting dynamics. Either way, stagnation prevents growth. Pastors must stay informed and attentive to shifting dynamics. They must keep up!

However, balance is necessary. Some pastors overcorrect by chasing every new trend that emerges in the church world. They move from one movement to the next, constantly shifting direction in hopes of staying relevant. Instead of establishing stability, they create an environment that lacks consistency, making meaningful growth nearly impossible. Congregations need clarity in vision, and an erratic leadership style prevents them from fully rooting themselves in the ministry.

Finally, when discussing matters of church growth, we must consider that a church will grow no larger than its leadership. If a pastor is not committed to continual learning and spiritual growth, the congregation will reflect that stagnation. Members look to their pastor as their primary source of spiritual nourishment, and if the leader ceases to develop, the church stops growing as well.

The Importance of Radical Hospitality

Radical hospitality begins with ensuring that every person who walks into the church is overwhelmed by the love of God. However, it cannot be performative; it must stem from a genuine place—one where there is sincere care and deep concern for people. One of the core teachings of the church is helping individuals recognize the value of one another.

At its heart, hospitality is about seeing people. One of the most profound questions we ask in life is, "Do you see me?" That question is central to what the church must embody. A welcoming atmosphere is created when both longtime members and newcomers alike, regardless of educational background or socioeconomic status, feel loved and valued. They must know they bring something unique to the church and are an essential part of the community. Pastors and leaders must be intentional about cultivating this environment, making sure that no one feels invisible or insignificant.

One of the most impactful changes that helped to grow our church was upgrading and expanding our hospitality ministry. The first face someone sees when they walk through the door matters. That smiling face, that warm handshake, that reassuring word of welcome—all of it sets the tone for their experience. A strong hospitality ministry tells visitors, "I am glad that you are here, and I am here to serve you!" It creates an atmosphere where people feel seen and appreciated. The goal is for them to leave having had a mind-blowing experience—one that sticks with them long after they walk out the door.

The follow-up process is just as important. When guests return for another visit, taking a moment to acknowledge them personally makes a difference. A simple statement like, "I knew you were here, and we hope you come again," reinforces that their presence is noticed and valued. Then, follow-up communication after their visit lets them know, "If you are searching for a church home, we want you to consider us." These small gestures may seem insignificant, but they leave a lasting impact that helps people feel welcomed and embraced. That's radical hospitality.

Training Members and Leaders to Extend Hospitality

Teaching hospitality begins with structured instruction, but the most powerful lesson on how to be hospitable in ministry comes through modeling. Training sessions can provide guidance, but there is no stronger method than pastors and leaders demonstrating hospitality themselves. A significant amount of learning happens through spiritual osmosis—being in the right environment and witnessing it firsthand.

I, in fact, learned the importance of hospitality by watching my pastor. While it is true that I have been blessed to receive formal theological training—and God knows that education has shaped me—nothing has influenced me and my skills in being hospitable more than observing my pastor in action. Bishop David Ellis and Bishop James David Nelson Sr. were masterful at navigating their congregations with radical hospitality. Neither of them was not formally trained, and neither was I. However, they had a deep understanding of people, a natural ability to lead, and a heart that cared. If you can train your hospitality team using these same characteristics, helping them to understand the critical connection between hospitality and church growth, your church will benefit—and grow all the more for it.

Creating a Culture of Worship

Worship stands at the core of the church's purpose. When God freed Israel from bondage, He did not do so merely for their liberation—He did it so they could worship Him. When Moses confronted Pharaoh, the call was for Israel to be released so they could hold a feast unto the Lord in the wilderness. Worship is not an afterthought in salvation; it is the reason for it.

God does not deliver people from sin without purpose. He calls them out so that they might honor Him with their lives, and that is the highest calling of the church: to worship and praise God (Exodus 8:1). This is the very reason creation exists. Worship is not just one element of church life; it is the foundation upon which everything else is built. In fact, I believe that this is one area of church life that pastors should remain actively involved in. They must pay attention to every aspect of worship, from what is being sung, to how worship is flowing, to how people are received and welcomed by the hospitality ministry—and everything in between. Most importantly, they must ensure that the presence of God remains the central focus of every gathering.

Worship must always remain centered on God rather than human display. The senior pastor sets the tone for worship within the church, serving as its guiding force even if they are not musically inclined. The pastor does not need to be a musician, but they must be attuned to the voice of God and committed to worship themselves. A pastor who embodies worship creates an atmosphere where it flourishes throughout the congregation.

Worship services should be spirit-driven. While order and preparation are valuable, there must always be space for God to redirect the service as He desires. This is particularly significant in Pentecostal settings, where openness to divine shifts is a defining characteristic.

It is my belief that pastors should remain responsible for and engaged in the planning and execution of worship services. They should never disengage and leave the planning of and responsibility for worship up to others in the church, because worship is at the core of the congregants' experience with the church. It is far too important and is too significant a part of the church experience to be handed off entirely. Pastoral involvement—selecting hymns, scriptures, and ensuring alignment between the music and the message—helps preserve a worship environment that remains spiritually sensitive. Asking the praise team what they are preparing to sing and occasionally redirecting selections ensures that the service remains in tune with what God is speaking to the church. The pastor should always have a hand in these aspects of ministry, even if in an oversight and approval role.

The pastor must also ensure that worship leadership practices spiritual awareness. While skill and preparation matter, true worship cannot be taught through mere instruction; it is cultivated through practice and submission to God's presence. Those leading worship should be reminded that their role is not to draw attention to themselves but to guide people into encountering God. Even small details—like attire—play a role in maintaining a proper focus. While certain styles may not be inherently inappropriate, anything that shifts attention away from worship and onto the individual must be addressed. The goal of worship leadership is not to impress but to create a space where people can seek God without distraction.

Altogether, the goal of pastors and the worship team leadership should be to make a spiritual impact above mere public recognition. A preacher should prefer hearing "The Lord spoke to me today" over "You preached that sermon." A singer should want to hear "I was delivered in praise and worship" rather than "You sang beautifully." John 4:23 reminds us that true worship must be in spirit and in truth, and those directing worship must pursue spiritual depth in every aspect of their ministry. In order to accomplish this, worship must be participatory, not performative. The role of the praise team is not simply to sing; it is to invite the congregation into worship. If songs are chosen based solely on vocal ability and complexity, they may impress listeners but fail to engage the congregation. This is also why worship should be accessible; if only the praise team can sing the song, then worship has become a performance rather than an invitation. Ultimately, the goal is not for people to admire the sound but to join in the experience.

When worship leaders open the door for full congregational participation, the church moves beyond watching worship to entering into worship.

Identifying and Equipping New Leaders

Selecting the right people for ministry leadership requires more than just skill; it demands spiritual depth and genuine character. When building a leadership team, prioritize individuals who exhibit a passion for God, a love for God's people, spiritual gifts, and practical skills. A team member must not only be talented but deeply committed to the kingdom's work.

Beyond ability, authenticity matters. Look for leaders who have a sincere relationship with God and a genuine love for people. Ministry is not simply about performing tasks; it is about serving with integrity and compassion. Equally important is a person's ability to work well with others. Leadership requires collaboration, and those who struggle with interpersonal relationships may not be suited for ministry roles.

Then, consider the purpose for which the leader is needed. In Titus 1:5, Paul states, "For this cause left I thee in Crete, that thou shouldest set in order the things that are wanting." I often reference this scripture when installing a pastor, as it serves as a reminder of purpose. The first lesson in leadership is understanding that God places leaders in position because there is a need. He never calls anyone into the pastoral office without clear purpose. Leaders must be careful not to resent the need because the need is the reason they are where they are.

When you are on a quest to identify leaders, be careful not to expect perfection from them, as that only sets you up for frustration and disappointment. Be willing to work with them and continually invest time in developing them on their leadership journey. Many frustrations in ministry stem from dealing with the imperfections of people. But it is precisely because people need guidance that pastors and leaders are placed in their roles. The responsibility of leadership is not to avoid challenges but to engage with them, knowing the work is meant to shape and perfect both the leader and those whom they serve.

I firmly believe that ministry is not just about perfecting others; it is also about perfecting the leader as well. The very things leaders encounter while guiding others often serve as lessons for their own growth. What God allows leaders to see in the people they shepherd, He also uses to shape and refine them in their own spiritual journey.

Leadership Development

One of the key initiatives in our church is a leadership training institute. This institute is designed to ensure that anyone aspiring to leadership undergoes a structured process that provides them with a foundational understanding of what it means to lead in the kingdom of God. Every ministry should establish a formal module that potential leaders must go through, allowing them to be properly equipped for their calling.

In addition to structured training, we hold monthly leadership meetings for all leaders within the church. These meetings are not just about exchanging information or aligning schedules; they serve as an ongoing form of continuing education. Leadership development is an active process, and these gatherings reinforce essential traits and qualities that should define those who step into leadership roles. These meetings also ensure that leaders remain current and adaptable in an ever-changing ministry environment. The importance of this cannot be overstated.

Dealing with Leadership Gaps

Leadership gaps can be tricky to navigate, and sometimes the best decision is to leave the space vacant rather than fill it prematurely. However, there are situations where certain roles are so vital that they must be filled, even if temporarily. In cases where an immediate replacement is necessary, a gifted leader who understands the importance of the position may need to step in as an interim solution.

Leadership vacancies require discernment. Yes, waiting on God to send the right person is ideal, but ministry often involves managing the reality of the moment. When there is an urgent need, finding a short-term solution can prevent unnecessary disruptions. It is like having a flat tire: you may need to put a temporary donut on just to get to the dealership where a full replacement can be made. Some positions can remain vacant until the right person arrives, while others require stopgap measures to keep things moving forward. In certain situations, a pastor may even have to step in personally to fill the gap until a suitable leader can be identified.

Delegating Responsibility

Leaders often ask how I choose to delegate responsibility in my ministry. My approach to delegating roles and responsibilities to leaders is informed by both spiritual guidance and practical organization. I believe in structuring the church like a business, ensuring that leadership responsibilities are clearly defined. As pastors and leaders, we sit down and develop an organizational chart, outline job descriptions, and strategically place different aspects of ministry into the hands of capable individuals. Accountability is essential, whether the role is fulfilled by a paid staff member or a non-paid leader.

One key distinction I make is eliminating the term "volunteer" from our system. Some pastors use the term, but I do not. If someone is engaged in ministry, they are not merely volunteering; they are fulfilling a calling and a responsibility. I actively work to disabuse members of the mindset that serving in church is simply doing God a favor. Ministry service is a sacred responsibility, and it should be approached with intentionality and commitment.

My church's structure is designed with different lines of responsibility, ensuring all roles report back and remain accountable to central leadership. This is where the leadership council and staff come into play. Their roles overlap but remain distinct, allowing for effective delegation. We continually encourage leaders to delegate responsibilities within their own teams, though it is often a challenge. For example, one approach we use is placing inexperienced individuals under the mentorship of seasoned leaders, to help them gain their footing and grow into the role. Rather than simply assigning leadership roles and walking away, we believe in maintaining ongoing lines of accountability to ensure that leaders grow into their responsibilities.

Maintaining Unity Within the Team

A unified ministry team thrives on honesty and transparency. Leaders must be upfront with their team, ensuring they consistently model open communication and ethical decision-making. Strong teams operate with a commitment to integrity, and it is crucial to insist on ethical behavior at all levels of leadership.

Another consideration in maintaining unity among a leadership team is that it is essential to avoid infighting, or internal conflict. Infighting within the leadership weakens the church's effectiveness, and a divided leadership sets a poor example for the congregation. One of the most damaging forces in ministry is unresolved tension among leaders, and pastors must take a firm stance against it. When disagreement arises, the goal should always be resolution before it leads to deeper fractures. Address issues early by bringing the team together for honest dialogue. A leader must both encourage unity and model it, demonstrating a spirit of reconciliation and cooperation. When unity is prioritized, differences can be approached with grace rather than hostility.

Regular meetings also foster connection, clarity, and unity, keeping everyone on the same page. Do not simply rely on occasional check-ins, but prioritize consistent interaction that you facilitate among leaders.

When dysfunction arises to threaten unity, and it inevitably will, confront it promptly rather than allowing division to fester. A strong leadership team is built on ongoing dialogue, mutual accountability, and a commitment to serving in harmony. Disunity breeds dysfunction, and when the pieces of a church are not working together, progress becomes impossible.

Unity is not a one-time achievement; it is a continuous effort that requires reinforcement. If God is not the author of confusion, then disunity comes from a different source. Leaders must be vigilant in ensuring that division is not allowed to take root. Thus, unity must be consistently emphasized. Paul reminds the church in his letters to remember key spiritual truths, reinforcing that some lessons must be repeated over and over again. The same applies to unity; it is not enough to teach it once and assume it will endure. Instead, leaders must keep the principle of unity at the forefront of their ministry, continually reminding their congregation of its importance. I'm aware that leaders often desire to always be fresh and revelatory in their teachings. However, foundational truths like this need to be reiterated and never neglected, because due to human nature, we are naturally prone to forget. Unity is one of those truths that must be echoed continually, both in words and in practice.

Ultimately, remember this: unity does not require uniformity. This is a principle that every congregation must embrace. Diversity within the body of Christ is a strength, not a weakness! Everyone—from bishops to pastors to lay members—must recognize that differences in perspective do not have to lead to division. Instead, they can contribute to a richer, more dynamic church community.

Incorporating Young Adults Into the Church's Future

Young adults play a vital role in the future of the church's leadership. In fact, they do not have to wait for the future; they should be actively involved now. I firmly believe that leadership positions should not be restricted by age. A person does not need to be 90 years old to serve as a deacon. Over time, I have worked to correct the mistake of sidelining young leaders, making a concerted effort to find positions for them within the church.

We have also made strides in incorporating young people into worship. Instead of separating them into their own setting, we engage them in corporate worship, allowing them to lead aspects of the service alongside the entire congregation. This initiative has been strengthened through our collaboration with the Lilly Foundation, which has helped facilitate intergenerational engagement in worship. By integrating young leaders into the broader service, we bridge generational gaps and ensure that they feel connected to the life and systems of the church. Young people are indeed the future, but they must also be actively involved in shaping the church in the present.

Developing and Empowering the Next Generation of Leaders

Cultivating the next generation of leaders amidst the current generation of leaders requires creating a team-oriented mindset rather than a competitive atmosphere. Leaders, both of the current and the next generation, must embrace the reality that everyone has different strengths. It is not about proving who is more capable; it is about recognizing that each person brings unique gifts and perspectives to the ministry.

I encourage you to teach both your veteran leaders and up-and-coming leaders in your leadership pipeline that their strengths are meant to complement, not compete with, one another. Instead of striving to outshine one another, leaders should focus on augmenting each other's abilities for the greater good of the ministry. Keeping the kingdom at the forefront is essential in order for the blending of leaders from different generations to work and walk in unity. If leaders remain focused on why they serve, personal ambitions and rivalry will fade into the background. The church must actively reinforce the principle that service is not about recognition; it is about fulfilling God's purpose.

Many churches have lost sight of this principle, and it is something that must be recaptured in ministry leadership. Leaders serve to build the kingdom, not to seek status. A ministry flourishes when leaders understand that their work is about collective impact, not individual acknowledgment. Thus, regardless of who is doing the work, whether seasoned veterans or next-generation leaders, what matters most is that the work is getting done. Encourage the seasoned, tenured members to keep working and do what is necessary to develop and deploy the next-generation members into leadership.

Our approach to mentoring and empowering young leaders is rooted in training and exposure. In addition to spiritual instruction, we prioritize providing opportunities for the next generation to engage with the broader world. We host college fairs and college tours, ensuring that young people receive guidance in their educational and professional pursuits alongside their faith development.

We have also established partnerships with local universities, creating avenues for young leaders to grow beyond traditional church settings. Through KAM University and our 10x10 program, we provide structured training to help young people develop leadership skills and deepen their spiritual foundation. While we do not mandate professional training, we encourage next-generation leaders to pursue educational and vocational opportunities that align with their calling. By equipping young adults with both spiritual and practical resources, we ensure they're equipped to lead not only in the future, but in the present.

CHAPTER 9

THE CHURCH IN THE COMMUNITY

Interaction with Other Congregations

One of the biggest mistakes new pastors make when entering a city is failing to establish relationships with other pastors and churches. If connections are not made early, ministry can quickly become isolating and unnecessarily difficult. The transition into a new community should be approached strategically. Young pastors often overlook a critical step when they start a new ministry: identifying and reaching out to the spiritual fathers of the city. Every region has established leaders who have served faithfully over time, shaping the spiritual climate. Understanding who these generals are and the dynamics of the ministry community they have helped to build helps new pastors integrate smoothly, avoiding unnecessary tension or misunderstanding. Ministry becomes far more fruitful when you have friends in the city rather than adversaries.

Equally important is developing ministerial ethics when interacting with other pastors. Unfortunately, there is a significant lack of pastoral ethics when it comes to how leaders regard, speak of, and engage with one another. It is far too common to sit in a room with pastors and hear them tearing down their colleagues in ministry. Such behavior erodes trust, damages relationships, and fuels unnecessary competition.

How do pastors navigate this culture without falling into its pitfalls? The first step is to operate with integrity and discretion. What you say about your fellow pastors matters. How you handle interactions with them sets the tone for your own ministry and credibility. If you want to remain trustworthy, your reputation must reflect honor toward others—even in disagreement.

Staying Engaged with Your Community

Early in my pastoral journey, I made it a priority to study the lives of seasoned leaders who exemplified excellence in community engagement. Among the foremost was the late Bishop David Lee Ellis, whose ministry left an indelible mark on me. He stood alongside contemporaries like Bishop Robert W. McMurry and Bishop Arthur M. Brazier—each a towering example of how to bridge the sacred and the civic, the sanctuary and the streets. These men were not only peers but also prototypes of what it meant to pastor with both spiritual conviction and community conscience. Their example profoundly shaped my approach as I stepped into ministry.

Growing up, Bishop Hancock was a community activist in his own way, though I was too young at the time to fully grasp the breadth of his work. As I matured in ministry, I realized that leadership requires stepping out of the church and engaging with the world beyond its walls. Pastors must get to know their community leaders and break out of what I call the "sanctified bubble," especially within Pentecostal circles. Historically, Pentecostals have often isolated themselves, fearing contamination by worldly influences. Yet, in doing so, we often forget our assignment, our role as influencers. Jesus called us to be salt, and salt must be applied; it cannot remain separate.

The only way to truly understand a community is to be present in it. Pastors must actively engage in local events, not just for participation but for meaningful connection. Invite the community into your church, build relationships, and ensure that your church has an active role in external affairs. Every congregation should have a community ministry dedicated solely to outreach—connecting with local residents, government officials, and advocacy groups.

I never imagined I would lead a social justice ministry, yet over time, I found myself building that arm of our church. Social justice is essential because inequality still exists in 2025. Many injustices persist in our world and culture, and we must recognize that one of Jesus Christ's primary missions was to minister to the disenfranchised. They need a voice, and the church must be willing to speak on their behalf. Keeping these issues before the saints and addressing them publicly expands our impact beyond the sanctuary.

Early in my pastorate, I did not fully understand the importance of community engagement, and I regret that. I was trained to remain separate, believing that staying within the church was the best way to preserve spiritual integrity. However, that approach did not serve me well.

Over time, I learned how to step outside, interact with leaders, and build connections that strengthened both our ministry and our influence. Our greatest impact often happens outside of the walls of our church.

Building Bridges with Local Leaders

Pastors who want to build bridges with local leaders must take the time to meet and interact with them. While ministry is demanding and pastors are busy, this effort is crucial for long-term effectiveness. In the early stages of building a church, much of this work must be done personally. However, as the ministry grows, pastors must delegate responsibilities to trusted individuals who can establish and maintain those relationships.

Every church should have tentacles—trained leaders, or ambassadors, who cultivate connections on behalf of the pastor. These individuals keep the church name active in the community, ensuring that the congregation is visible and engaged in meaningful initiatives. They represent the church, build relationships, and create opportunities for the pastor to strategically step in when their presence is most needed. By establishing a strong network of trusted voices, the church maintains influence without requiring the pastor to personally manage every external connection.

When done correctly, this approach allows the community to see the church in action. It is not enough to preach about social issues or leadership—we must actively participate in shaping the community. When local leaders recognize the church as a contributing force, doors open for greater collaboration, influence, and impact.

CHAPTER 10

FINALLY, MY BRETHREN

As pastors, we have been entrusted with one of the greatest responsibilities: to shepherd God's people with wisdom, integrity, and love. Ministry is not about titles, positions, or accolades. It is about the lives we touch, the people we help grow in faith, and the moments when someone looks at us and says, "Pastor, you helped me." That is what makes this work fulfilling, not the applause or the recognition, but the transformation we witness in the lives of those we serve.

But let's be honest: this calling is not easy. You will face challenges, moments of exhaustion, seasons of uncertainty. There will be times when you wrestle with surrender, when you wonder if you are making an impact, when leadership feels heavier than you imagined. In those moments, remember this: your strength is found in staying connected to God. If you don't remain in His presence, you will run on empty. If you don't allow yourself to be fed, you will pour out without replenishment. Never get too comfortable leading that you allow yourself to forget that you, too, must be led.

You will be responsible for maintaining unity in the church, discerning God's will in difficult seasons, keeping your team aligned with the vision, and ensuring worship remains centered on Him. You will need to strike the balance between inspiration and information, leading with conviction while remaining open to growth. You must stay humble enough to hear wisdom even from unexpected voices, and bold enough to stand firm when God calls you to deliver a difficult word.

And through all of this, never forget the reason you were called: to help people walk closer with God, to guide them through their struggles, to be a steady voice of truth and encouragement. The success of your ministry is not found in numbers but in those whose lives have been changed because of your obedience to God's call.

As you step into leadership, do not walk alone. Surround yourself with wise counsel, remain open to the Spirit's leading, and most importantly, never lose sight of the joy found in serving God's people. This is not just a role—it is a sacred assignment. Lead well, love deeply, and let God shape the impact you leave behind. You are stepping into something greater than yourself, so trust Him to guide you every step of the way.

Bishop is praying for you.

www.ingramcontent.com/pod-product-compliance
Lightning Source LLC
Chambersburg PA
CBHW060956230426
43665CB00015B/2221